Positive Reinforcement for Kids:

A Basic Guide to Understanding and Practice

C. Patrick Cliver

Dedicated to my wonderful sons, Andrew and Alex.

I thought they were brought into my life so that I may teach them, but little did I know, it was the other way around.

Disclaimer:

Positive Reinforcement for Kids:

A Basic Guide to Understanding and Practice

Table of Content

Contents

PREFACE:

Positive Reinforcement is one of those rare things that almost everyone thinks they know what it is and yet they do not. Almost everyone also intuitively feels it is a good thing. These same people have always meant to implement it with their kids but just never got around to it. When they hear the term Positive Reinforcement they perk up and applaud it but never do much beyond that. The purpose of this book is to get you beyond that so that you really know what it is and why it would or would not be good for your children. It should help you get to a point where you will either start implementing it or decide once and for all that it would not be right for your children.

That last sentence may have surprised you so I should explain it a bit. This is NOT the Positive Reinforcement manifesto and we will not be talking about how every person in the world who interacts with children should be using Positive Reinforcement for every child. Hear this now. Positive Reinforcement may not be right for you or your child. In fact, even if it is, it is not going be right for every situation you encounter.

Positive Reinforcement is a tool for your parenting, teaching, coaching, or whatever toolbox and is not a dogmatic philosophy that one must convert to in order to make it work. Hammers are not the best tool for screws and not all kids are going to be screws (nor, of course, am I implying that you should hit your kids). What I mean is, different kids require different techniques so as a Parent it is helpful to be able to try as many different techniques as possible so you can find the one, or ones, that work best for your child or children.

While I'm not an academic, I have extensively educated myself in the field of Positive Reinforcement for kids as a parent of a special needs child and professionally, am an expert in the use of Positive Reinforcement on adults. Let me take a step back. I am not psychiatrist, psychologist, therapist, counselor, or licensed professional, in any field that would qualify me to give professional therapeutic counseling or diagnosis. I'm stating this as a positive thing though because Positive Reinforcement, as a concept has a very academic background and I think this has made it less accessible to the non-academic trying to do the right things for their family.

My purpose in writing this book is to educate people as to what Positive Reinforcement really is so that they can make some informed decisions for themselves. The purpose is not to make you feel bad if you do not use Positive Reinforcement or tell you that it is the right way and all other techniques are the wrong way. This book came about because, as a parent, I had constantly been trying to find all the information I could on the subject and had been frustrated. What I found was either over simplistic or too academic with no practical middle ground. That is what I strive to create here, a practical middle ground accessible to all us Caregivers who have questions.

About me: I mentioned that I was not a parenting expert but, I do feel that I have become an expert Parent. That doesn't mean I don't make plenty of mistakes and don't have plenty of room for improvement. What I feel it means is, that I have worked hard to be a better Parent than I was and I try to use my many mistakes as educational moments to learn lessons so they are not wasted. The good news is this book is not about advice, it's about taking this complex concept of Positive Reinforcement and making it understandable to as many Parents and other adults who work with children as possible.

I have two sons, ages fifteen (Andrew) and nine (Alex). My eldest has Asperger Syndrome, which is often called high functioning Autism. Autism is what they call a "spectrum Disorder" which means that how it manifests itself is not always black and white. Imagine writing down thirty symptoms (for lack of a better term) on pieces of paper and sticking them in a hat. Now pick eight pieces of paper out and roll a die. If it comes up six stop, but otherwise pick another piece of paper and repeat until you either roll a six, or have all 30 pieces of paper. Now for each piece of paper, spin a wheel with the numbers 1-100 on to determine the severity of each symptom.

Congratulations, in the role-playing game of Autism you just created a character child with Autism. As you can imagine, this creates a lot of variation and it's hard to find two children affected in exactly the same way or have it impact their life in exactly the same manner. That is the spectrum and different kids end up on different parts of it. Given that, you can imagine that parenting must be adjusted to conform with the special needs of these children and, although they have many differences, one thing that many of them have in common is that Positive Reinforcement seems to works pretty well with them. It has, and does, work very well with my fifteen year old "Aspie".

So you are saying, well, I'm glad that Positive Reinforcement worked for you and your child but, my child doesn't have an Autism Spectrum Disorder. Well, let me also tell you that many A D H D Asperger children are misdiagnosed, and Andrew was no exception. We knew he was different as early as when he was four years old. We took him to see experts including a psychologist who diagnosed him with ADHD. We of course had never even heard of Asperger Syndrome at that point but came to find out many years later this misdiagnosis is common in Aspies. Well, we were referred to a psychiatrist who also supported this diagnosis and prescribed ADHD medication. We educated ourselves and came to find out that Positive Reinforcement works exceptionally well for many kids with ADHD. This was our first exposure to Positive Reinforcement.

Well, you may say now, I know there are millions of kids diagnosed with ADHD and Asperger Syndrome but my child has neither. My child doesn't either. To be more exact, my youngest child doesn't have either and, by virtue of fairness and ease of parenting, we have used Positive Reinforcement with him as well and, guess what, it works fantastically with him too. He is a gifted child in the top 5% of his class and is very different in many ways from his brother. Again, this is not to say that Positive Reinforcement works for all children, but my non-medical, professional opinion is that it can work for most kids that don't' have Asperger Syndrome or ADHD just as I have seen in my professional career working with adults of all stripes. This book will hopefully be helpful for Parents who fall into this category, who do not have access to the professionals and the resources that come with having children with these challenges.

I also have some expertise in creating incentive programs. When you start reading about Positive Reinforcement you inevitably come across the concept of incentives or Rewards, which can be implemented in some kind of system like a "Token Economy", where children earn tickets that can be traded in for another Reward. Think of arcades where kids win tickets for the games they play and turn them in for trinkets or toys at a prize counter. Professionally, I worked with fortune 500 companies setting up "Token Economies" for their employees, suppliers, partners and customers which we called incentive programs.

That may sound crazy in that context but let me ask you, do you have a credit card that gives you points or some kind of miles for making purchases? That is an incentive program for adults. Use your card to buys things and get reinforced with points that you redeem for Rewards. Another example would be the top sales people earning a trip somewhere or an employee going above and beyond, earning a bonus. An even more common example of this is your weekly paycheck. As an incentive to get you to do X,Y, and Z your employer tells you they will pay you a sum of money every two weeks, or whatever time interval. You do your job and you get paid. You do not do your job and you stop getting paid. There is an "incentive" for people to do X, Y and Z, and so it gets done.

So, as you see, Positive Reinforcement programs are all around us as adults and we don't think twice about them in our lives. Positive Reinforcement programs are promoted for kids diagnosed with Asperger Syndrome and ADHD. Doesn't it make sense to at least look at Positive Reinforcement as a potential parenting strategy for the rest of those kids out there for whom it may, or may not, work for? They are going to be exposed to them as adults anyway. In any case, it is up to you as a Parent to make these choices and to know your child well enough to know what works. What you will find here is an explanation of what Positive Reinforcement is in a down to earth way with real-world examples.

I hope this book is as informative and helpful as it was intended to be.

CHAPTER 1:

What is Positive Reinforcement?

Most People think they know what Positive Reinforcement is. Some people have pets and know about it as a dog training technique. Some people with kids have heard the term bandied about by a teacher or in some school setting. Some people know about it because of some psychology class somewhere. Some people just intuitively know what it is even if they didn't know the name. Maybe it's because the name is pretty self-descriptive. Do people really know what it is? Do you? Really? Let's find out.

1) Bobby is eleven. His Mom told him that he would be rewarded by not having to do his chores on days he brings home a test with at least a B grade.

<u>Is this an example of Positive Reinforcement?</u>

2) Maria's Mom wanted her to do her chores after school. To motivate Maria, her Mom made her an Ice cream sundae right when she got home from school. She did this every day for 2 weeks and not only did Maria gain weight, she did her chores on 2 more days than she had done in the two-week period prior to the daily Reward.

Is this an example of Positive Reinforcement?

3) Lee was 3 years old and loved to throw food while at the table. On average, he threw food at one meal per day. Lee's Dad decided to try something. Every time Lee threw food while at the table, he was put into the corner for 3 minutes. After a week of this, Lee was now throwing food at two meals per day on average!

Is this an example of Positive Reinforcement?

4) Kevin was the coach of his son's little league team. The kids were not hitting the ball very well, so he decided to try something new. Before each child got up to bat, Kevin pulled them aside and told them something positive like "I know you can do this" or "I believe in you". He did this for every batter every time they got up to bat. Sure enough, the kids batting average when up as a team over the course of the next week.

Is this an example of Positive Reinforcement?

5) **Coach Kevin, from the team above, had to quit and so Coach Sara took his place. She wasn't sure this was working so instead of telling each player something positive every time before they batted, she decided to encourage them if only if they did not get a hit, when they returned to the dugout. Sure enough, over the course of the next two games the kids got more hits.**

Is this an example of Positive Reinforcement?

I'm sure you are dying to know how you did, but before I let you see the answers, you have to promise to come back and keep reading as this is just a simple quiz to see what you are bringing to the table. OK, go to the end of this chapter and you will find the answers.

Click here to go check and come back with your results.

Welcome back. Did you get them all right? You weren't supposed to, so if you did, kudos to you but keep in mind, we are just scratching the surface here. If you got some wrong, don't feel bad, most people get all or most of them wrong. Now you have probably re-read the questions and are ready to defend you answers. This is where I'm supposed to tell you why the answers are different from what you thought they should be.

I will do that later in the book, in the parts relevant to each of the questions. If I just told you why right now, you would have the answer without the understanding. Think of this as motivation to read the rest of the book. If you read on, then you will be rewarded with the answers to the questions you have right now.

Let take a step back and start with a definition of Positive Reinforcement. All kinds of sources have definitions, and they vary a good deal, which made selecting one a challenge. Here is a simple definition from Wikipedia:

"Positive Reinforcement: the adding of an Appetitive stimulus to increase a certain Behavior or Response."

3

(*Wikipedia 2011*)

So the next thing I had to do was find a definition for Appetitive stimulus, so I checked Wikipedia and it had the following:

"Appetitive stimulus: a pleasant outcome" (*Wikipedia 2011*)

From Wiktionary (www.thefreedictionary.com) we find that the word "outcome" is defined as follows:
outcome (plural outcomes) Information, event, object or state of being produced as a result or consequence of a plan, process, accident, effort or other similar action or occurrence.

The definition does not specify the who or what that Positive Reinforcement can be used on, but we are only concerned with children and we bring with us at least the expectation, if not the knowledge that it can be used with children, so we will confine it to them.

So we can rewrite the definition to simplify it for our needs like this:

Positive Reinforcement for Kids: The adding of a pleasant result or consequence, to increase a certain Behavior or Response in a child or children.

OK, that sounds a little less clinical.

What is implied in the wording is that there is an actor, a person performing the Positive Reinforcement (the adding), that is either the same person or has the same desire for the

4

Behavior or Response as the person adding the pleasant result or consequence. That person can be a Parent, a teacher or whoever but for our purposes, will be an adult in charge of children. Let's just call that person a Caregiver as an all-encompassing term for all those people.

So basically it is a Caregiver using a Reward to get a child to do something they want them to do. That may be an oversimplification but it's a good place to start.

Results of the quiz

1) Not Positive Reinforcement
2) Not Positive Reinforcement
3) Is Positive Reinforcement
4) Not Positive Reinforcement
5) Not Positive Reinforcement

CHAPTER 2:

Positive Reinforcement as a Tool

A lot of people have a preconceived notion about what Positive Reinforcement is because the term has entered our collective vocabulary, but unfortunately, not the definition. People have been known to mythologize and idealize ideas that are new to them and this can sometimes happen when someone starts learning a little about Positive Reinforcement and experiences some success with it. Have you ever known someone who just heard about a new business opportunity, or discovered something within their religion, or took a new class, and they had become fanatical about it? They talk about it all the time and saw elements of it in all they did as if it is then the glasses through which they view the world. They became passionate about it, and that can be a great thing.

I feel I am passionate about Positive Reinforcement, but I try very hard not to let that cloud my judgment. It is important to keep perspective as to what it is capable of, when it is appropriate and when it is not working. When you see first-hand a technique working so well with your child it is easy to want to use it in every circumstance, but as Abraham Maslow said, "If you only have a hammer, you tend to see every problem as a nail". Don't get me wrong, Positive

Reinforcement is amazing, but it is not a cure all and not the beginning and end point of parenting.

Positive Reinforcement is a tool for the parental toolbox. If you want to build a solid, well rounded table that can support itself and carry the weight of the items it is meant to bear, you will have much more success if you use a variety of tools such as saw, a level, a drill etc. If you tried to build a table with just a saw, even the best saw ever made, at the end of the day you will just have a stack of wood and not a table. Positive Reinforcement is an excellent tool, but if Caregivers don't also use the other tools at their disposal, they will end up with a beautiful stack of wood that can be eaten off of but is not a table.

When I first started using some of the techniques we will discuss later on, it worked with my child. That may not be a very stirring statement but you have to understand that I was lost. My son was diagnosed with severe ADHD at the age of four. Some Parents come to parenting with a lifetime of experience from having had brothers and sisters, babysitting, or even working with children. I was an only child who never interacted with a child who wasn't a peer until I was a father. I had this wonderful little boy who didn't act like I thought he was going to, but I really didn't have a baseline for comparison other than my own childhood memories.

Andrew was a puzzle to me. He was thrown out of multiple preschools and generally didn't play well with others. He was smart and funny but also very immature and goofy, verging on weird. I know that sounds horrible coming from his father, but it's honest. He was a little weird sometimes and lacked imagination. Of course, I love him with all my heart, but I had a hard time relating to him. Getting him to do the things that other kids do with a little prodding just didn't work with Andrew. I tried Punishments from time outs to taking things away even to spanking. The latter is something I had said I would not do but when all else fails you go with what your Parents did because you rationalize that you turned out alright.

None of it worked. Much of it led to us butting heads, temper tantrums, and melt downs, some even from Andrew (wink). It was frustrating not being able to get my child to do simple things. Early on he had several developmental delays including being slow to walk and talk. By age four we knew he was not like other kids and so we had him tested. He was diagnosed with severe ADHD, and they recommended medication. I fought the diagnosis and especially the medication. I educated myself about ADHD, and I let the "experts" talk me into the medicine. It worked in a lot of ways but was certainly no cure all. There is much more

ADHD

A developmental disorder in which a person has a persistent pattern of impulsiveness and inattention, with or without a component of hyperactivity.

to this part of the story, but that is for another book.

Reading up on ADHD is where I first came across Positive Reinforcement, and it has been a part of my vocabulary ever since. This was the first technique that worked with Andrew, and I became a fanatic with Positive Reinforcement as my religion. And why not? It worked so effectively and in so many circumstances that I built our daily routines around it. There were times it didn't work, but I told myself that I did it wrong or the incentive was not a motivating enough one or something was wrong with my implementation. It took quite a while for me to assess that the issue was with me and that I was seeing the world though Positive Reinforcement glasses.

Positive Reinforcement worked and still works extremely well, but once I started using it with other parenting techniques, I became a more effective Parent. Better still, because I was no longer a one trick pony, when I used Positive Reinforcement, which was still quite often, it worked even more effectively. This was important because, as you probably know and I discovered, as we become better Parents, children get older and more complicated, making you a less effective Parent. It is a constant game of one-upmanship. You do your best to stay even with the curve.

Andrew had some tough times and when he was ten, after some traumatic incidences that I won't go into here, we discovered that he had been misdiagnosed, and in fact, actually has Asperger Syndrome. It was like having a light turned on but also like starting from scratch as everything I learned about ADHD was pretty much null and void. Everything, except for what I knew about Positive Reinforcement, which still applied because it also works as well with children with Asperger Syndrome. We had our foundation and that made the re-education process that I had to begin much more bearable. As of this writing, Andrew is a teenager and is doing great.

Asperger Syndrome

"is an Autism Spectrum Disorder that is characterized by significant difficulties in social interaction, along with restricted and repetitive patterns of behavior and interests. It differs from other Autism Spectrum Disorders by its relative preservation of linguistic and cognitive development. Although not required for diagnosis, physical clumsiness and atypical use of language are frequently reported."

Many of you may be thinking, well this is great, but my kid doesn't have either of these conditions so does that mean Positive Reinforcement will not work for my child? I have another son as well. Alex is six years younger than Andrew, and he does not have ADHD or Asperger Syndrome. If fact, other than being gifted intellectually, he is pretty normal. We started using Positive Reinforcement with Andrew before Alex was born. By the time he got older, it had made sense to try it with him as well since he saw us use it with his brother and there was a matter of fairness. Well, to make a long story short, it worked with him, as well.

We don't use Positive Reinforcement the same with our two boys, not even adjusting for age. What was appropriate for Andrew at age six was not appropriate for Alex at age six. The beauty is that there is no rigid system, so we could apply the techniques even though we were reinforcing totally different Behaviors for a very different child. No two children are the same so something that works on one child may not work as effectively, or even at all, on another child.

The important takeaway is that it worked as an effective parenting tool with Alex. I have seen it work very effectively with all sorts of children who are otherwise "normal", as well as, children with conditions or challenges. If you think this is only for kids with special needs then you should look at the education system. Positive Reinforcement is used, on purpose, in classrooms throughout the world. Teachers long ago discovered how effective Positive Reinforcement is and have been using it with our children, with great success, for decades.

Positive Reinforcement is used to great effect ever day on almost all adults as well, but that is a topic for another chapter. The point is that Positive Reinforcement is a fantastic parenting tool that can be used on a large variety of kids with varying degrees of success, but generally speaking it is very effective for most kids. It is also not the end all be all for our interactions with our children. Caregivers should learn about and use every effective tool and stick with the ones that are right for the child in their circumstance. Parents and Caregivers who develop their system to fit the child will more likely be successful than the ones who try and fit the child to the system.

CHAPTER 3:

A Brief History of Positive Reinforcement

This is not a history text so relax, we aren't going too far into the history of it. Having said that, it is important to know your roots, so to speak. It will be helpful for us to explain how we got to where we are with modern Positive Reinforcement theory.

Most of you are probably familiar with Pavlov's dog. For those of you who aren't, here is a brief synopsis. Ivan Pavlov was a Russian scientist back in the 1920's. He discovered that if he rang a bell right before giving a dog some meat powder it would "condition" it to  associate the bell with the food. After enough times, he found that simply ringing the bell would cause the dog to salivate.

 This was an important discovery as it led to new line of study he defined as Classical Conditioning. To be more precise, it describes a type of learning that animals, and as was later discovered, humans, exhibit. To describe what was going on, Pavlov created some terminology including unconditional and conditioned stimulus, as well as, unconditional and conditioned Response. To understand what these mean it may be helpful to replace the term "unconditional" with the phrase "naturally occurring" and replace "conditioned" with "learned, trained or taught".

So let first look at what was happening before Pavlov introduces anything. The dog would see food and salivate. This is what happens naturally, so the term unconditional will be used to describe the process. The food is what stimulates the Behavior, so that will be our Unconditional Stimulus which then causes the unconditioned Response from the dog in the form of salivation. Next he rang the bell when the food was presented so the dog learned to associate food with the bell sound until it got to the point where just the sound of the bell, even without the food being present, caused the dog to salivate. In the final scenario, salivating to the sound of a bell had been learned by the animal so that the bell was the conditional Stimulus and the act of salivating to a bell, as opposed to food, was the conditioned Response.

The next person of note is Edward L. Thorndike. Edward L. Thorndike (1874–1949), was a psychologist and scientist who advanced the study of Operant Conditioning. He is probably most famous for formulating his "Law of Effect". This law basically states that Behaviors that result in a pleasant result or outcome are more likely to happen in the future while conversely, Behaviors that result on an unpleasant result or outcome are less likely to occur in the future.

Thorndike came to this conclusion by conducting a series of

16

experiments over time using cats and Puzzle boxes. Basically he put together some contraptions that entrapped the cats in a box with ropes, obstacles, levers, etc. so the cats had to perform a specific action or series of actions to get out of the box. When a cat would perform the correct sequence, not only would they get out, they would receive food.

Thorndike observed the actions of the cats and timed how long it took them to perform the correct actions to gain their release and food. He discovered that the cats randomly did things until the stumbled across the Behavior that would lead to their release from the Puzzle box, and when they were reintroduced to the box, it would take them less time and the Behaviors that did not lead to their release were tried less. This pattern was repeated with different cats and all of them figured out how to get out to the food in less and less time, and less trial and error. So the Behaviors that led to escape and food were more likely to be repeated and those that didn't were less likely to be repeated.

The next important figure in the history of Positive Reinforcement is Psychologist John Watson (1878–1958). Watson is the father of the school of psychology known as Behaviorism. The sciences distinguish themselves as something unique in that they can not only describe the world but also make predictions about what will happen and then go one step further and set up a test in order to see if the prediction is accurate. To this point in history, psychology had dealt with the inner working of the subjects and was quite subjective. Watson intended to get outside the mind of the subject and look at the Behaviors they exhibited. His goal was to bring a more scientific base to the discipline of psychology.

He wasn't concerned with our thoughts, emotions, genetics or any subjective influences on human Behavior, as they cannot be objectively be measured, or in some instances, even known. His desire was to take psychology a step closer to a "hard" science such as chemistry which can be proven experimentally, without subjective influences and only that which is observable, verifiable and repeatable. He wanted to be able to take this information and then make predictions about human Behavior.

Watson saw Behaviors in terms of cause and effect or more precisely, Stimulus and Response. This would define the science of Behaviorism and came to be known as the S>>R model. He sought to find the most basic stimuli and their Response in order to establish the cause effect relationship and make predictions and saw this as the basic component of study in this science. He saw more complex Behavior as simply a combination of this basic stimuli and Responses. He saw Responses as simply an organism's learned way of reacting to its interaction with the environment and Conditioning was simply that process by which it learned to react to a new stimuli, or learned a new Response to a known stimuli. Some believe that all Behavior is a product of this Conditioning and others ascribe preconditioning to inheritance, whether it be social, such as a lioness training it's cub to hunt, or that cub naturally exploring a desire to hunt leading up to this because of "instinct" or genetics.

John Watson famously said that if you gave him a dozen infants, and a controlled environment, that he could raise them to be anything from a skilled professional to a beggar on the street or even a criminal. This boast is legendary in the field of psychology and is pretty much discussed in every introductory course on the subject. We are all familiar with the nature vs. nurture argument, and this represents the pinnacle of the nurture side of this debate. The other side of course is the more Darwinian camp and of the opinion that our genes will determine our outcome no matter what the environment or social circumstances. We generally ascribe a more middle of the road opinion now, recognizing the contributions of both nature and nurture working in combination.

Next in our family tree comes B.F. Skinner (1904-1990), who we can consider the father of Positive Reinforcement. Watson influenced the entire generation of psychologists after him and Skinner was no exception. He started from Watson's work and expanded it as well as correct some areas that fell short. A model on Behavior that is limited to just stimuli and Responses possess a problem because it does not explain what happens when there is no stimuli and gives the organism only reaction without motivations or independent actions. Skinner took Watson's work to the next level by acknowledging these things and seeing that organism's future Behavior depends on what happened to when it performed that Behavior in the past.

Watson practically denied the mind existed while Skinner did not, he simply made the observation that it was not practical to study the mind when we have observable, quantifiable events known as Behavior in which to study. To pursue his studies Skinner took another page from Watson's book and created his own sort of Puzzle boxes which were called Operant Chambers, but also came to be known as Skinner Boxes. Much like the Puzzle boxes, an animal was Rewarded with food when it discovered the correct lever or trigger from the gadgets within the chamber. Like Watson's cats, Skinner's rats and pigeons would stumble on the trigger, get the food and then become more proficient at repeating the Behavior necessary to getting more food.

He further studied these animals and how they reacted to variations of this scenario, observing what happens to Behavior when different stimuli are added or removed. He paid attention to which Behaviors were strengthened or weakened and why. Through these observations, he came up with the language of Operant Conditioning that we use today including Positive Reinforcement, Negative Reinforcement, Positive Punishment and Negative Punishment. Positive and negative referred to whether a Stimulus was added or taken away and Reinforcement referred to the strengthening of Behavior while Punishment referred to the weakening of a Behavior. Skinner had a most profound influence on Behaviorism and brought the discipline to the consciousness of society where is still resides today.

These four men are not the only contributors in the history of ideas that Positive Reinforcement draws its lineage from, but they played a significant part. Pavlov identified Classical Conditioning with his experiments on dogs. Thorndike built on that work and came up with Law of Effect by observing cats in Puzzle boxes who learned to escape faster each trial.

Watson rejected the study of the internal life of organisms as they were not objectively quantifiable, and instead focused on observable Behaviors or basically anything that organism does as an action as opposed to what it may think or feel.

Finally, Skinner synthesized these ideas and coined the term Operant Conditioning to describe the causes of actions and their consequences. Skinner and his work will be emphasized more going forward as we discuss Reinforcement principals and specifically Positive Reinforcement. There is important work done by people after Skinner, the post Skinnerians if you will, but we will only lightly touch on that as it goes beyond the goal of this work, which is to give a basic and thorough understanding of what is Positive Reinforcement for Kids in theory and practice.

Before we go any further, there is a minor point we need to hash out. Whether you believe in the theory of evolution or not, I hope we can agree that animals in some ways are very much like humans. This can be seen in Behaviors such as how certain animals care for their young or toolmaking Behaviors in monkeys or hundreds of other subtle ways. Not surprisingly, Positive Reinforcement is used with success on certain animals ranging from dogs to seals to monkeys. It can also be shown that physiologically, some animals are very similar as well which is why we conduct lab experiments on rats and transplant baboon hearts to humans.

Does any of this mean that anyone is suggesting that your children should be "trained" like a pet? Of course not, that would be ridiculous. Feeding and caring for young are things that animals do but that doesn't make your son a cocker spaniel because you feed and care for him. Baby animals play just as our children play, but that doesn't make them kittens. Just because the principals of Reinforcement at the basic level work for humans, as well as some animals, that doesn't degrade the human any more than sharing the ability to learn degrades a human or the ability to vocalize that we share with some animals degrades us.

Again, I'm not looking to debate these issues, but I just wanted to throw these topics out there so hopefully they don't become issues. We have seen how Positive Reinforcement was discovered by way of a line of animal studies, and indeed you

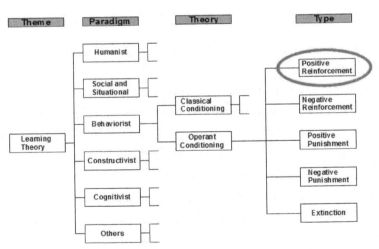

can find dog training courses built around the basic principles of Reinforcement. Yes, it is effective for training animals to learn certain Behaviors but depending on what animals you are talking about, there is never anything more than that. For humans, learning the Behavior is simply the first step toward building habits, learning discipline, understanding complex concepts, as well as, building character.

If Jack won't stop hitting his sister, it will be difficult to focus on other topics. Let's face it, as Parents you can only spend so many waking hours of the day with your children and you want to maximize that time with them. If you spend your day yelling at Jack for hitting his sister and punishing him, you end up with an angry son, hurt daughter, and frustrated Parent. The Behavior is controlling the day, the people and what they are focusing on. If the Parent used Positive Reinforcement to control the problem Behavior, then the day could be used to address the underlying cause of why Jack is hitting. You could instead spend time teaching lessons of empathy or building the brother sister relationship or to just having fun. The Parent then controls the day, the people and what they are focused on.

CHAPTER 4:

Operant Conditioning and Reinforcement, an Overview

There is a lot of confusion over the terminology used with regard to Positive Reinforcement. It stems from being rooted in the academic subject, psychology, loaded with a lot of technical jargon designed by accident or on purpose, to keep the laymen, (us) at arm's length. We tend to think of Positive Reinforcement as this entire big philosophical movement all alone in its own section of psychology and parenting. The first thing we must realize is that by focusing in on Positive Reinforcement we are actually jumping into one subtype of a type of learning. It's kind of like we are explaining the concept of eating to an alien that doesn't eat and we tell them about at the restaurant experience but keep bumping into terms about the cooking process, farming and food shopping.

We need to back away for a moment and look at what we are discussing from the trunk of the tree and then work our way out to the branch. Let's start with the general theme within the Psychology of Learning Theory. Within that theme, there are several overarching paradigms, one of which is Behaviorism. Behaviorism itself has a number of theories within it, with the two predominant ones being Classical Conditioning and

Operant Conditioning (a.k.a. Radical Behaviorism). Operant Conditioning can be further broken down into five types, one of which is Positive Reinforcement. (See diagram)

So Positive Reinforcement is one type of method within Operant Conditioning, which is one theory of Behaviorism, which itself is one of several paradigms within the theme of Learning Theory, which again is one of many themes within the Subject of Psychology. This is not supposed to make Positive Reinforcement seem unimportant. It is important. The purpose of this is to give you some perspective. Positive Reinforcement is not a religion or philosophy or way of life or even a parenting theory as some would have you think.

Positive Reinforcement is one of the means of changing Behavior as described in the theory of Operant Conditioning put forth by B.F. Skinner based on his work and the work of others before him including Pavlov, Thorndike, and Watson. So again, we are talking about a method for changing Behavior. Keep that thought in the back of your head throughout the rest of this book. I think we have taken some of the mysticism away from Positive Reinforcement and brought the concept back down to earth, but I also think there is tremendous power in that. As long as we remember that it is just a means of changing Behavior and not some miraculous cure-all that will transform a problem child into something they are not, then there is much that can be accomplished with it.

Now that we have narrowed the scope of what Positive Reinforcement does, let's talk about changing Behavior. As Parents and Caregivers, a good part of what we do is focused on creating or changing Behaviors in children. We do a lot more, such as instill values, set an example, provide opportunity, educate them etc., etc. Behavior change can be a challenge, and can take up a good part of our Caregiver time and capital if we let it and thus, take away from the other areas of care giving. The introduction of Positive Reinforcement for one or a handful of Behaviors can become a framework for dealing with future Behaviors. Once in use, the underlying principles of the system are understood by the children and Caregivers alike and new Behaviors can be addressed directly and promptly without a learning curve, misunderstandings, or reinvention of the wheel each time.

NOTE: A quick note about terminology here. For the remainder of the book, I will be using the term "Caregivers" as opposed to just Parents, or Parents and Caregivers, or any combination of titles and terms used to cover people who watch or contribute to the raising of children. While not all Caregivers are Parents, all Parents, who are involved with their children, are Caregivers, so that is the term I will use. If I mean to specify, I will say Parent, or Coach, or Babysitter, or what have you, as the situation dictates.

Now that we have Positive Reinforcement in perspective, let's take a step back. Operant Conditioning is a process of learning by which the Behaviors an organism performed in the past may be used to predict future Behaviors of the organism. It assumes that Behaviors that resulted in pleasant outcomes will be more likely to be repeated while Behaviors that resulted in unpleasant outcomes will be less likely to be repeated.

Here, is a quick review of what the difference is between Classical Conditioning and Operant Conditioning. Classical Conditioning involves already existing biological Responses being associated with new stimuli. A classically conditioned dog would still just drool, but they would just drool more often as more stimuli evoke this Response. Operant Conditioning involves new or different Responses (learning) to stimuli based on the past outcomes of Responses to the same or similar stimuli. A dog trained with Operant Conditioning can not only drool but has also learned to roll over on command because this Behavior was reinforced with a pleasant outcome such as a treat often enough for it to be learned.

An example of Classical Conditioning: Your new dog loves to go on trips with you and gets very excited when you put him into the car to go somewhere. One day you start jingling your keys as you are putting him in the car. You do this the next couple times you take him somewhere. The next time, you start jingling your keys in the house, and your dog gets all excited as if he was just put in the car because he has been conditioned to relate that sound to the event of the car ride, which makes him happy.

Basically, you are doing something different that elicits the same Response from your dog.

Here, is an example of Operant Conditioning: Same dog, loves to go for rides in the car. In this instance, you are house training the dog, and whenever he does his business outside, you immediately take him to the car and give him a quick ride. After a while, the dog makes the connection and the incidence of the dog doing his business outside increases (as opposed to inside).

In other words, the dog is doing something different that elicits a Response from you that, in turn, is pleasing to the dog and it effects the desired change in the dog's Behavior.

Sometimes these theories are talked about in terms of Stimulus (S) and Response (R). Operant Conditioning is more of a chain of stimuli and Responses (R > S > R) whereas Classical Conditioning is more represented by a single Stimulus and Response (S > R). This is because, in Classical Conditioning the Response does not change whereas in Operant Conditioning the Response is dependent on the outcome of the previous Responses of the organism. So, we can say

Operant Conditioning

-Positive Reinforcement
-Negative Reinforcement
-Positive Punishment
-Negative Punishment
-Extinction

the Stimulus drives the next Response in Classical Conditioning, and the Response determines the next Stimulus in Operant Conditioning.

In our first example, a new S was introduced (key jingling) and associated to the existing S that elicited the same R from the dog (excitement). In the second example, when a (desired) R occurred (dog doing business outside) a pleasant S was introduced. So you can look at Classical Conditioning as a new way to bring about the same Behavior whereas Operant Conditioning increased the likelihood of a new, and/or preferred Behavior occurring. So, if it is Behavior change you are seeking, Operant Conditioning is the way to go.

Operant Conditioning has five components including Positive Reinforcement and Negative Reinforcement which strengthen Behaviors as well as Positive Punishment, Negative Punishment and Extinction, which weaken Behaviors.

Positive Reinforcement is the (+) adding of a pleasant Stimulus in order to strengthen a Behavior. For example, a child does her homework by a certain time and is allowed extra play time.

Negative Reinforcement is the (-) subtraction of an unpleasant Stimulus in order to strengthen a Behavior. For example, an irritating buzzer goes off in your car until you put on your seat belt at which time the noise is removed.

<u>CHAPTER 1 QUIZ ANSWER</u>

I promised an explanation of the quiz questions in chapter 1. I will explain them in as the concepts arise naturally in the book.

1) Bobby is eleven. His Mom told him that he would be rewarded by not having to do his chores on days he brings home a test with at least a B grade.

Is this an example of positive reinforcement?

The answer was no.

Many of you said yes and may have been tripped up by the word Rewarded. Many of us have learned to associate Reward with positive reinforcement but as this proves, that is not always the case

Positive = Adding Something

Bobby's Mom took away or "subtracted" his his chores and it strengthened the desired behavior of getting good test grades. So this is an example of Negative Reinforcement.

It could be argued that this is intended Negative Reinforcement because we don't know if the desired behavior actually increased in frequency or not.

Positive Punishment is the (+) addition of an unpleasant Stimulus in order to weaken a Behavior. For example, a little boy pulls a dog's tail and gets bitten thereby reducing the chance he will pull a dog's tail again.

Negative Punishment is the (-) subtraction of a pleasant

Stimulus in order to weaken Behavior. For example, a child continues to break a household rule as so her parents remove the TV from her room.

Extinction is when Reinforcement has been removed, and the frequency of the Behavior decreases because of that.

We will review each of these types in more detail in the chapters to come but just to give you a basic understanding for now, I will review the five components of Operant Conditioning. Setting aside Extinction for a moment, many of you will be tempted to group the positive with positive and the negative with the negative. You must resist and group Reinforcement with Reinforcement and Punishment with Punishment. Think of the negative and positive like you do in mathematics as opposed to attitude, correctness or moral connotations these words may bring to mind.

CHAPTER 5:

Reinforcement and Punishment 101

We understand a little about Operant Conditioning now so let's examine its types a little closer. Again, we are talking about Positive Reinforcement, Negative Reinforcement, Positive Punishment, Negative Punishment and finally Extinction. We are going to discuss Extinction a little later so right now let's break it down into Reinforcement and Punishment.

I had a lot of trouble understanding which of these were which until I had the breakthrough of forgetting what I thought I knew and learning the simple meaning of each word that makes up the types. The first thing I had to do was free my mind from the preconceived notions of Positive and Negative that I brought with me. We want to see Positive as good and Negative as bad. Throw these thoughts out and think about it as if it was purely mathematical. Think positive as in a plus sign and negative as in a minus sign.

Reinforcement = To Strengthen a Behavior
Punishment = To Weaken a Behavior

Positive = Adding Something
Negative = Subtracting Something

Once I remembered these four definitions I never had trouble again. That meant forgetting most of what I thought Positive Reinforcement was and everything about what I thought Punishment was. I had always associated Positive Reinforcement with Rewards, as in things. Punishment I always associated with consequence and retribution. These associations were not all that helpful in this context.

So, let's practice our new skill and look at the Behavior and the consequence of the following situations:

Situation: Take away a toy because the child hit his playmate. Type: Taking away the toy is subtracting something so we know it's Negative. A child hitting his playmate is a Behavior we would want to weaken so this is going to be Negative Punishment if it does so.

Situation: A child receives a gold star on their quiz paper for getting an A.
Type: The gold star is added to the child's paper and the Behavior is one that we would want to strengthen so this would be Positive Reinforcement if it does strengthen it.

Situation: A child was caught talking in class and was made to stay after school and clean desks.
Type: The Behavior is talking, which is one we would want to weaken, and the consequence was a task being added to the child's to do list, so it is Positive Punishment.
Remember, don't be a slave to language and our preconceived notions of "Positive" and "Negative"

Situation: A child who had been struggling with manners was exceptional one night, so his Parents relieved him of his normal job of clearing the table.

Type: The consequence was to take away an unpleasant task because of the display of a Behavior they wanted to encourage so this would be Negative Reinforcement.

These can be tough, especially Negative Reinforcement and Positive Punishment because the words just want to grate on our sensibilities. They just don't sound right as if they are an oxymoron. Stick to our four basic definitions and you will get past this and be just fine.

Our terms Positive or Negative mean to add or subtract in the general sense but takes on a different meaning depending on whether it is paired with Reinforcement or Punishment as we must define what we are adding or subtracting. When the goal is to strengthen the Behavior, the child must receive something (Stimulus) they like, want, brings them pleasure, happiness or any combination of the four, so the promise of more encourages a repeat of the Behavior. The flip side would be that the child must have something they dislike, don't want, brings them pain, unhappiness or any combination of the four removed so that a repeat of the Behavior is encouraged and the thing (Stimulus) is kept from coming back.

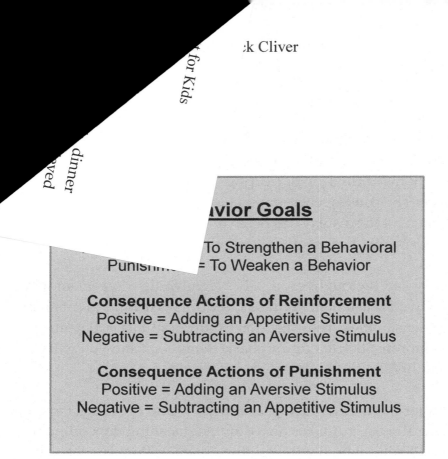

vior Goals

To Strengthen a Behavioral
Punish... = To Weaken a Behavior

Consequence Actions of Reinforcement
Positive = Adding an Appetitive Stimulus
Negative = Subtracting an Aversive Stimulus

Consequence Actions of Punishment
Positive = Adding an Aversive Stimulus
Negative = Subtracting an Appetitive Stimulus

It can get murky if we bring our own subjectivity into the equation. We must remember that what we think is aversive or appetitive is irrelevant. The only thing that is relevant is what the child receiving the Operant Conditioning thinks is aversive or appetitive, and the success or failure of the Conditioning may be the ultimate judge of that.

Example 1: Adding an hour of time to a child in their room by themselves. An extroverted social child would see this as aversive, while an introverted child may see this same Stimulus as appetitive.

CHAPTER 1 QUIZ ANSWER

I promised an explanation of the quiz questions in chapter 1. I will explain them in as the concepts arise naturally in the book.

3) Lee was 3 years old and loved to throw food while at the table. On average, he threw food at one meal per day. Lee's Dad decided to try something. Every time Lee threw food while at the table he was put into the corner for 3 minutes. After a week of this, Lee was now throwing food at two meals per day on average!

Is this an example of positive reinforcement?

The answer was yes.

Many of you said no because this sounds like a time out which is supposed to be a punishing action. What is aversive to some is appetitive to others and this stimuli acted as a reinforcer as it encouraged a measurable increase in the behavior of throwing food. Unfortunately that was not the behavior they wanted address and they were looking to do punishment as opposed to reinforcement.

Remember that outcomes are a better judge of what is aversive and what is appetitive to a child.

Example 2: Subtracting cauliflower from a child's dinner. Again, the child who hates cauliflower sees it as aversive while another child who loves it sees the exact same Stimulus as appetitive

As you see, appetitive or aversive is in the eyes of the beholder.

Stimuli
"Appetitive stimulus = a pleasant outcome
Aversive stimulus = an unpleasant outcome" (Wikipedia)

When we say "pleasant outcome" and "unpleasant outcome" we are simply saying something the subject of the Behavior change likes or doesn't like the outcome. This is of course very subjective to the person being reinforced, and so that is why the word "outcome" is used since it the outcome of the presentation of the thing to the subject and not the thing itself that determines if it is an Appetitive, Aversive or Neutral outcome. One child may be ecstatic with a doll while another child may be insulted by it. Same item, different outcome.

Now let's start from the beginning knowing our preconceived notions won't trip us up. When we use the term Reinforcement we are describing a particular kind of consequence that follows a Response by an organism that works to encourage the increase or frequency of that Response to that given Stimulus. The Reinforcing consequence can come in a variety of forms and can vary in effectiveness between two otherwise very similar beings. People tend to gravitate toward anything that will bring them pleasure and move away from that which brings pain. This is the proverbial carrot and stick. Reinforcement plays off this dichotomy by offering to increase the carrots and/or decrease the sticks if the organism chooses to perform the Behavior that is being reinforced.

Skinner chose to view Reinforcers, the consequence itself, in terms the subject defined. What I mean by that is he did not seek universals, and that is because there are no universals when it comes to what we find pleasant and what we find unpleasant. When looking at humanity as a whole, can you say chocolate is always a pleasant consequence and burnt toast is always an unpleasant consequence? Of course not because in a world of billions of people there are people who don't like chocolate and there may even be people who are allergic or have a severe negative reaction to it. The same goes with burnt toast. If even one person finds that pleasant, can we still say it is an unpleasant consequence? Skinner used the approach of being neutral with regard to the Reinforcer and introducing it with the mindset of letting the subject define the Reinforcing value based on the strength of the Response and the amount of strengthening or weakening it did to the Behavior in question.

Skinner experimented with Negative Reinforcement, as well. He used electrified Skinner Boxes that delivered an unpleasant shock to the subject rats until they hit the proper lever. Once they accidentally discovered the correct lever they would hit it faster with each time they were introduced to the box. Hitting the lever removed the unpleasant Stimulus of the electric shock so that hitting the lever was the Behavior that was strengthened in the rat. This type of learning is also known as escape learning but is a prime example of Negative Reinforcement. He even set up a light as a warning indicator that the shock was about to come. The rats learned this relationship and went for the lever even before the shock arrived and demonstrated, what is also known as, avoidance learning.

We won't be shocking any children, of course, but these are clear-cut examples that help us understand Negative Reinforcement. Clear-cut examples are important because it can be confusing to distinguish positive from Negative Reinforcement and can often come down to how you want to look at it. For example, Charlie is 13 and has been told he can go outside and play if he completes his homework before 5pm. Assuming he does so, and the consequence leads to a strengthening of this Behavior, the question then is, was the Behavior of doing his homework by a certain time positively reinforced when he was allowed to go outside to play, or was it negatively reinforced when he was no longer restricted to the house? You can twist this around on almost every example you can come up with, but at the end of the day, does it matter? What is important is the desired Behavior was reinforced and therefore, strengthened.

Punishment, on the other hand, works by reducing the strength of a Behavior. Punishment can be thought of as the opposite of Reinforcement as it weakens Behavior while Reinforcement strengthens Behavior. This is a dangerous comparison though because even though they work in opposite directions they are not equals in effectiveness. Skinner determined that Reinforcement was much more successful at both changing Behavior, and once changed, the successfulness of the change. In other words, Punishment may change the Behavior of the subject, but once the Punishment is removed, the Behavior weakens much faster than in the case of Reinforcement. So, if you are looking to create more permanent Behavior change then Reinforcement is a better bet.

So again we have a scientific base for Operant Conditioning as you can measure Response strength and whether the Behavior is strengthened or weakened over time. That which you can objectively track and measure can be tested and predicted. There is the cause and the effect that is seen in play with other sciences. The cause is the desired Behavior and the effect is the pleasant outcome which then becomes the cause for a repeat of the effect and so on. So Positive Reinforcement is any consequence, that when presented after a Behavior, strengthens that Behavior, or in other words, increases the likelihood that that Behavior, as opposed to others, will be repeated. The relationship must exist such that the Reinforcer comes after the Behavior, and because of the Reinforcer, the Behavior is strengthened.

So let's take what we have covered here and further refine our definition of Positive Reinforcement and add definitions for the 3 other forms of Reinforcement and Punishment to help us come to a better understanding of all four.

<u>Working Definitions</u>

Positive Reinforcement for Kids: The adding of a result or consequence that the child finds pleasant, dependent on the occurrence of a certain behavior or response by the child, which results in an increase in the likelihood of that behavior or response in the child, because of the added result or consequence.

Negative Reinforcement for Kids: The removal of a result or consequence that the child finds unpleasant, dependent on the occurrence of a certain behavior or response by the child, which results in an increase in the likelihood of that behavior or response in the child, because of the removed result or consequence.

Positive Punishment for Children: The adding of a result or consequence that the child finds unpleasant, dependent on the occurrence of a certain behavior or response by the child, which results in a decrease in the likelihood of that behavior or response in the child, because of the added result or consequence.

Negative Punishment for Children: The removal of a result or consequence that the child finds pleasant, dependent on the occurrence of a certain behavior or response by the child, which results in a decrease in the likelihood of that behavior or response in the child, because of the removed result or consequence.

CHAPTER 6:

Reinforcers

We now know a little about Operant Conditioning and that Reinforcement is the attempt to strengthen a Behavior while Punishment is the attempt to weaken a Behavior. We know that in this context, Positive means to add a Stimulus and Negative means to take a Stimulus away. We will focus on our primary subject of Positive Reinforcement as we are now going to discuss the stimuli that are added with the intent of strengthening a target Behavior which are also known as Reinforcers.

We have touched on positive Reinforcers already, and we know that they are a consequence that follows a Behavior that increases the likelihood that particular Behavior will be repeated. Positive Reinforcers can be anything because it is the child that determines what is, or is not, a positive Reinforcer through their future Behavior, or more specifically, the repetition of the Behavior that was reinforced with a greater frequency that it was performed without the Reinforcer. Of course, the key here is an increase in the target Behavior because if it occurs just as frequently as before, then the consequence was not a positive Reinforcer. If the frequency of the Behavior actually decreases because of the Reinforcer, then you actually have a Punisher instead of a

Reinforcer.

Things get a little dicey here as well with the positive and negative monikers. A Reinforcer is a consequence that results in the Behavior being reinforced, thus strengthening it or increasing its frequency. If it is a positive Reinforcer, it is something that will be presented to the child while a negative Reinforcer will be something that is taken away. Which is a better positive Reinforcer, a peanut butter cup or a bag or rocks? If you said bag of rocks, then you are wrong. If you said peanut butter cup don't pat yourself on the back too quickly because you are wrong too. These are just two neutral things and will remain that until presented to a specific child after a specific Behavior and then through a repetition of Reinforcement with this thing in question we see an increase in that Behavior. At this point it is magically transformed from a mere thing to a positive Reinforcer.....for _that_ child. Most of us would find the candy Reinforcing and the bag of rocks not so much so, but what matters to us does not matter in Positive Reinforcement. What matters in Reinforcement is what matters to the child being reinforced. My youngest son used to be allergic to peanut butter, and although he outgrew that, he is not a fan of peanut butter, but as a collector or rocks and minerals he would be a happy to get a bag of rocks.

It is important that we let the results tell us what we need to do next when we are trying new and different Reinforcers. You are an expert on your child, and you may very well know more about them than you do about yourself. Use this knowledge as advantage and be careful to not let it become a blinder that hides a wall you may end up crashing into. Use your knowledge to know what to try, but don't suppose your knowledge will tell you what will work, let the results do that. You may think junior is the biggest baseball fan in the world and end up being baffled when your child's Behavior does not change. You may think he has a Behavioral problem or at the very least is being defiant. Then again you may take a step back and let the results bring you to the conclusion that junior loves you but is not especially enthusiastic about baseball. Children often do things for a myriad of reasons including to please their parents, get their attention or just spend time with them. Make sure the Reinforcers you use are Reinforcing to them and not you.

For example, let's say you want a child to remember to wash their hands without being asked before dinner. When the child sits at the table with clean hands you give the child a page from a coloring book on a topic they like.

The coloring book page is a Positive Reinforcer, True or False?

Most of you probably answered true which, unfortunately, is not the correct answer. False is not the correct answer either as this is a trick question. The answer has to be that not enough information has been given to determine one way or another. The most important part of the definition of the Positive Reinforcer is that it increases the occurrence of the target Behavior.

If the child washes their hands more often after you start the practice of giving the pages, then it is a Positive Reinforcer. If the frequency of the Behavior is unchanged, it is not a positive Reinforcer, and if it actually decreases then it is a Positive Punisher. I know it's hard to think of giving a child a coloring page on a topic they like a Punishment, but remember we are leaving our preconceptions at the door and referring to our definition that a Punishment weakens a Behavior. Maybe the child likes the topic but hates coloring or maybe the child's art was criticized and now any thought of coloring makes them sad. As a Caregiver, you would want to probe into this but for our purposes it suffices that the Behavior was weakened and therefore it would be a Positive Punisher.

Negative Reinforcement is often confusing to people, primarily because the words sound like a synonym for Punishment. To further the confusion, when we think of taking something away it also sounds like Punishment at first but, not to beat a dead horse, think back to our definitions. We are removing an Aversive stimulus that results in an increase of the Behavior. A child hates to do their assigned daily chore of washing the pots and pans and for having shown up at the table with washed hands for a whole week straight, the Caregiver relieves them of dish washing duty that night, and this Reinforcer leads to another week straight of the desired Behavior. This would then be an example of Negative Reinforcement by its very definition of removing a Stimulus thereby increasing the likelihood of a Behavior.

Now that we have made some distinctions, we are now going

to discuss various forms of Positive Reinforcers. Remember throughout this book that when I talk about Reinforcers I am merely making suggestions when discussing anything even vaguely specific. What is or is not a Reinforcer is specific to each and every child. Let's say candy could be a Reinforcer to 99.9% of all children. That doesn't make candy a Positive Reinforcer for any particular child until it demonstrates an increase in the desired Behavior. This is even limited to likes versus dislikes as it can be situational as well. Candy may be a Positive Reinforcer to a child most of the year but maybe not when used as a Reinforcer three days after Halloween, or maybe not when the Behavior is getting out of bed in the morning and the child doesn't like candy in the morning. (I'm not suggesting that candy be given in the morning or even used as a Positive Reinforcer at all but simply trying to illustrate a point.)

For the rest of the book, when the term Reinforcer is used it should be implied that Positive Reinforcer is what is meant. If I refer to Negative Reinforcers, then I will write out the full term Negative Reinforcers.

Our first breakdown of Reinforcers distinguishes between Primary Reinforcers, also known as Unconditioned Reinforcers, and Secondary Reinforcers, also known as Conditioned Reinforcers. A Primary Reinforcer is something that is naturally reinforcing to that child. Thus the term Unconditioned Reinforcer makes sense as these are things that a child finds to naturally be an Appetitive stimulus (a Stimulus producing a pleasant outcome). Think back to Classical Conditioning and the dog drooling in Response to the sight of the food (Not saying kids are dogs here). The scientist didn't need to train or condition the dog to salivate over the sight of food, which came naturally. Speaking in generalities, we don't have to condition most children to love ice cream, playing a game, swimming in a pool, watching their favorite shows, or any number of other things. Primary Reinforcers are what motivate us.

Secondary Reinforcers have to be learned to be wanted. So  calling a Secondary Reinforcer a Conditioned Reinforcer makes sense because the child must be taught to associate the Secondary Reinforcer (i.e. a check on a chart which earns a Reinforcer once full) with the Primary Reinforcer it has been paired with (The Reinforcer the completed chart earns the child). Back to Pavlov, this is akin to the bell that was paired with the presentation of food. The bell meant nothing until the association with the food was taught or conditioned. A sticker chart with ten grid spaces means nothing until the child learns that ten stickers filling that grid means she will have earned the new toy which is the Primary Reinforcer. Another example is my child's dentist's office which gives each child a plastic coin if they survive the dental visit without a fit. That coin can be used in some machines each containing a variety of small toys.

Some Secondary Reinforcers fall into a category called Generalized Reinforcers. A Secondary Reinforcer is a placeholder or symbol for some Primary Reinforcer the child wants or would enjoy. A Generalized Reinforcer is a placeholder or symbol for a choice, that choice, being from amongst some number of Primary Reinforcers the child wants or would enjoy. The prime example of that is the Generalized Reinforcer we are all familiar with which is money. Money represents choice, in that we can trade it for what we want. Another example we'll cover more in a later chapter would be points earned by children that accumulate until they earn enough to redeem them for an item of predefined Primary Reinforcers in which to choose from. Have you started to notice that you are being reinforced in different areas of your life? As adults, of course, we earn money for certain Behaviors but aren't we also conditioned to earn points on our card or earn miles on this airline etc.?

There are several categories, if you will, of Reinforcers including Activity, Sensory, Tangible, and Social. A quick note, the goal is to have a child exhibit a particular Behavior with no outside, or Extrinsic Reinforcement, but rather have intrinsic, or internal, Reinforcement Reinforcer the activity. An example could be reading for the pure enjoyment of reading. Obviously, if a child is already intrinsically reinforced to perform a Behavior, a Caregiver should never mess that up by applying an Extrinsic Reinforcement. We can label this Natural reinforcement. Life is filled with natural Reinforcers like the crisp sweetness of a ripe apple to feeling great after a good workout. When natural Reinforcers are already in play, as the saying goes, if it ain't broke, don't fix it. Sometimes we may need to use Extrinsic Reinforcers to get a child to discover the natural Reinforcers they never knew existed.

Activity Reinforcers are simply activities that particular child would enjoy doing and couldn't just do on their own. These are "doing" Reinforcers where a child can participate in something they would enjoy. Again, speaking in generalities as what matters is what matters to the child in question. Some examples of these may be getting to play outside, being a member of a group that carries the flag at a ceremony. Another example would be getting to be the special helper or getting to play a game or go to the movies. One I see often at my kids' schools is special ice cream parties or movie days when the class performs a certain Behavior a certain number of times. There are untold numbers of different Activity Reinforcers and again, what makes it or any other thing mentioned below, a Reinforcer, is that it quantifiably increases the desired Behavior over time.

Tangible Reinforcers are basically "thing" Reinforcers. This can be a toy or a sticker or any item the child being reinforced would enjoy. Tangible Reinforcers are things and are often what are thought of as the Reinforcers when people think of Positive Reinforcement. Sensory Reinforcers are things that are pleasing to the senses including touch, smell, sight, hearing or taste. Examples would be letting a child listen to a favorite song, eat a special dessert, drink a soda, pet a soft stuffed animal or anything really that engages the senses.

Finally, Social Reinforcers are the things we find enjoyable that come from our relationships with other people including praise and recognition. For children, Social Reinforcers can come from adults or other children. Peer pressure works because kids value the Social Reinforcer of acceptance. Parents telling their children that they are proud of them for XYZ or a teacher acknowledging a student's hard work on a paper are other examples of Social Reinforcers.

These categories are not hard and fast by any stretch of the imagination. If you use a trip to the ice cream parlor as a Reinforcer, is it an activity or sensory? What if it is a downloaded song, is that tangible or sensory? Is an award certificate tangible or social? They are more just to help you think about different things that can be used to reinforce Behavior. As a Caregiver, it may be more productive to think of them in terms of three categories, cost, time and effort. When coming up with Reinforcers, take these three things into consideration when trying to match an appropriate Reinforcer to a Behavior. It is essential to make the Reinforcer substantial enough to motivate the child while also cheap enough not to break the bank. It also needs to be quick enough so you still have time to get other stuff done and easy enough that it doesn't become a second job.

As you can see, there are a wide assortment of Reinforcers available. Caregivers should approach the use of Reinforcers as they would food. Just because your child likes macaroni and cheese doesn't mean that's what you should serve them for breakfast, lunch and dinner  every day. Kids need a variety of foods for nutrition and to avoid boredom just as kids also need a variety of Reinforcement for better results, and to avoid boredom, as well. Just as Caregivers shouldn't use Positive Reinforcement as their only Parenting Tool, they shouldn't stick to one Reinforcer or even one category of Reinforcer

CHAPTER 7:
Extinction and Satiation

When we hear the word Extinction, images of dinosaurs and endangered species come to mind and in this context, it is Behavior. Imagine that you have a secret fishing hole and every time you go there you catch several fish. Then after several trips like that you have a trip where you don't catch a single fish. You attribute it to bad luck or something like that. Next time you still have no luck and assume it must be the bait or something else. You may stop fishing for a while or try out other spots so that you aren't going to the secret spot as much and eventually, you stop going altogether. Fishing in that spot is a Behavior that was reinforced with the catching of fish, and when that Reinforcement went away the Behavior decreased until it stopped.

Behaviorsaurus

If a child raises their hand in class, gets called on, and then gets praised for the correct answer, they will likely do that again. Let's say this child is getting all the answers and the teacher wants so encourage the other kids to participate so they stop calling on this child to answer. If they are not getting called on then the child will raise their hand less and less and if it continues, will stop raising their hand at all. We would say that the Behavior of hand raising was extinguished. Notice the child doesn't stop immediately after the first time they are not called, but persists in raising their hand for a while and slowly tapers off.

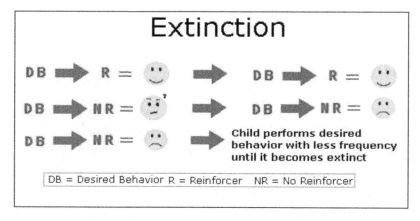

Sometimes a child will have seemingly stopped performing a Behavior, and then, without having received a Reinforcer, will start performing the Behavior again. This is called Spontaneous Recovery and it is like a last-ditch effort to make sure the Reinforcers are no longer being given for this Behavior. In the case of the fishing hole above, maybe you figure it's been a while and maybe you should give it another shot. When it doesn't pan out you may try to vary more things in an effort to make it work again. The child in the classroom may raise their hand again after a while to test the waters and see if they would be called, and thus have the Reinforcer return again. This experimentation is sometimes called an Extinction Burst.

Again, I know it's a little creepy sometimes to be discussing the Behaviors of rats with techniques we will ultimately be using with our children, but look past it. Imagine that you start coming to work early and your boss notices and compliments you. Your boss goes out of his/her way to mention how impressed they are, which pleases you because you really want a promotion. One day the boss doesn't say anything and, if fact, it wasn't just that day but every day. You are no longer catching the boss's eye, and the snooze button starts getting harder to avoid in the morning until you start coming in at your regular time. You still occasionally come in early to see what happens, but when the boss doesn't notice that you eventually stop all together. That is an example Extinction and Spontaneous Recovery.

Now let's say that Reinforcement has stopped for a given Behavior. The Behavior begins down the road to Extinction, and the process will continue as described, assuming the Behavior is never again reinforced. The question you may have is what happens if the Reinforcer is given even just once during the Extinction process. That is an excellent question and what happens is it reverses the Extinction process, and makes it take longer the next time the Reinforcement stops. If you

Reinforcement Schedules will be covered extensively in Chapter 8

reinforce the Behavior every time it is performed then the child will immediately recognize when it is stopped and the process of Extinction will immediately begin. If the Behavior is not reinforced every time, also known as Continuous reinforcement, the child recognizes this and when the Reinforcer is not presented it appears normal to the child and the Behavior continues. If the Reinforcement is not presented after each time the Behavior is performed it makes the Extinction process take much longer. This is called Resistance to extinction or Persistence. This is an important phenomena, and we will touch on this more when we discuss Schedules of Reinforcement later.

For example, let's say you want your child to do their homework before dinner time. To reinforce this Behavior you allow them to have an extra hour of time on the TV or computer when they do it. Every time they get their homework done by dinner time they earn the extra hour. To be sure they are not encouraged to lie about having homework, the deal only applies to nights when they have homework and you have to check it when they are done. One day, when they have completed their homework by dinner time, you explain to them that they have to come with you to their brother's soccer practice, and they aren't going to get their extra hour. Between practice and games, suddenly Monday through Friday, the days homework is assigned, are no longer available for the extra hour of TV or computer time and so the Reinforcement has stopped. The child may continue to do their homework by dinner time for a while, but then slowly but surely they regress to doing it later and later until it is never done before dinner time. The Behavior has become extinct.

Another example may be Reinforcing a child for cleaning their room well every two weeks. Your child does a great job

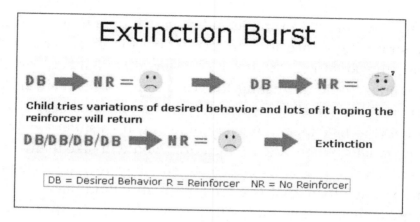

cleaning their room one day, and you make a big deal out of it and take them out for ice cream as you had agreed in advance if they made it spotless. Two weeks later the same thing and two weeks after that the same thing again. This goes on for a while until one cleaning day you are too busy to take them. They still do a great job next time, but for some reason you can't take them again. They do a good job next time as well and then nag you to take them for ice cream but you are again busy and tell them that cleaning their room is their job and you shouldn't have to take them for ice cream for doing their job. They still clean their room every two weeks because they have to but the effort slacks off to the point where they are doing a pretty poor job. Then, after a couple weeks of this, the child does a fantastic cleaning in a Spontaneous Recovery, maybe the best they ever did, and ask you to come look and marvel at it. You tell them that yes, they did a great job, but you don't take them for ice cream. The next couple weeks they slack off again and may have another Spontaneous Recovery and do a super cleaning a month down the line again. Assuming the ice cream Reinforcement never comes back, the over the top effort may become extinct.

If we take that last example and change it up a little, we can illustrate Resistance to extinction. Take the same situation with the Reinforcer of the ice cream after that first great cleaning. While out eating the ice cream, you explain how proud of the good work you are. You also explain that you are not able to take them out every time they do a super job, but occasionally, when you see the effort, you will take them out for ice cream. The next week comes and they do a super clean, and you tell them that you are busy and remind them that it is not an every time thing. The next time you take them and then it's three times after that one and then twice in a row. You remind them each time that it is not an every time thing. Something happens so you aren't able to take them for several room cleanings in a row. The child may continue to put in the extra effort for weeks or even months before slacking off, because not getting ice cream was not out of the ordinary and therefore was not an immediate signal that something has changed.

One of the things that get tricky here is that an argument could be made that what we are calling Extinction is Negative Punishment. Think about it. Your boss was providing an Appetitive stimulus, praise and recognition, and he/she took it away, which weakened your Behavior. That's sounds exactly like Negative Punishment. Technically speaking, it fits the same basic definition, but the difference is that Extinction is the removal of a Positive Reinforcer previously added with the intent of Positive Reinforcement, where Negative

Punishment is the removal of Reinforcer that was not previously associated with the Behavior, which is the target of weakening.

So we have talked about Extinction as it relates to Reinforcement which explains to us what it is and why it works. Now let's look at it on as its own as a separate component of Operant Conditioning. We know there is Reinforcement and Punishment, each with a positive and negative version, but we listed Extinction as the fifth component. Sometimes we want Extinction to happen. In a way, it is a strategy that does the same thing as Punishment and you have heard of it plenty of times, and had it recommended for dealing with various Behaviors. The concept of Extinction is really just another way of looking at the parenting technique of ignoring a Behavior. What we described above was an accidental side effect or a purposeful effort to wean a child off of Reinforcement. What if we stop delivering Reinforcement in a deliberate effort to cause a Behavior to become extinct?

For example, let's say your child wants some jelly beans and 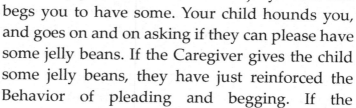 begs you to have some. Your child hounds you, and goes on and on asking if they can please have some jelly beans. If the Caregiver gives the child some jelly beans, they have just reinforced the Behavior of pleading and begging. If the Caregiver says no, then the Behavior should start to become extinct. As long as the Caregiver does not give in and consistently says no then the Behavior should go away. Now what I didn't say is that there must have been some history here of a Reinforcer in the past as a result of the undesired

Behavior of begging in order for the child to think the strategy will work and continue doing it. Just like the examples above, if the Caregiver gives in and allows the child a cookie even just one time they have now reinforced the Behavior again and created a Resistance to extinction.

We hear many experts tell us just ignore bad Behaviors and they will go away. What they don't always tell you is why this works and under what circumstances this does or does not work. First thing first, the Caregiver must sit down and examine the Behavior and the child's motivation for performing the Behavior. If a child is misbehaving because they crave attention and the negative attention is all they have been able to get, then ignoring the bad Behavior can cause it to become extinct. Hopefully the Caregiver will also find an acceptable way for the child to get attention from them. Ignoring Behaviors works when something you do as a reaction, is the the Reinforcer. If the child is being reinforced in some other way, then ignoring the Behavior will just insure that it persists.

To make a Behavior extinct, it is essential that the Reinforcer not be delivered after the Behavior is performed. If ignoring the Behavior is not eliminating the Reinforcer then you are in trouble because ignoring it is not going to work. It is vitally important as Caregivers for us to try and understand what is reinforcing a behavior. If a child is cracking jokes in class and you and the teacher decide to ignore it, the problem will persist if it is the laughter of their peers that is giving them their Reinforcement. Only by breaking that Reinforcement of their peers is there any chance of changing the Behavior. If the

64

teacher punished those kids who laughed in class or reinforced those who didn't, even if not seemingly fair, then they would be working to eliminate the class clown's Reinforcement so that the children stop laughing and the Behavior of joking in the classroom becomes extinct.

Satiation is what we call it when a Reinforcer starts to lose its effectiveness, which may cause Extinction to begin. It is kind of like getting too much of a good thing. If you love pizza, you

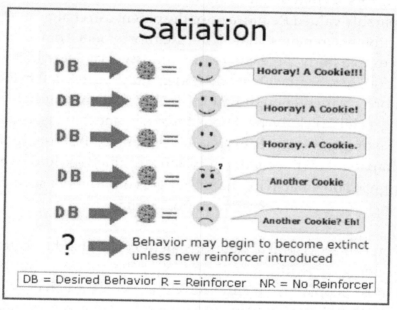

may get very excited and thrilled to have it one day. If you have it again the next day you would still like it, but maybe you aren't as excited. Thirty straight days of pizza and all but the really diehard fans would not only not be excited, but would not want to eat the pizza at all. If you are giving the same Reinforcer every day, then you should expect it to lose some of its appeal, and thus its effectiveness, in motivating your child.

There are several strategies for avoiding Satiation, some of which we will discuss in more detail later in the book including the use of a Token Economy. Another way to avoid Satiation is by not using Continuous reinforcement, and the alternatives to that are discussed in the chapter in Schedules of Reinforcement. Another strategy is to use varied Reinforcers so maybe the child can choose from a basket of comparably valued Reinforcers or the parent can change it up. The problem remains that if the Reinforcement comes too often even a fairly large choice of Reinforcers can get old and Satiation can begin. One other idea may be to make the Reinforcer varied enough that it is never the same twice like letting a child pick the next book for story time. Finally, it can be a Reinforcer in which, even if it is repetitive, the absence of it is impactful on the child. For instance letting the child earn the right to do an activity that never gets old to them such as playing on the computer for a period of time.

As you can see, Positive Reinforcement is not just the "catch them doing something good" and "give them a treat" model that most people mistakenly think it is. As a Caregiver, you need to have a goal, a plan, a way to measure progress, and the willingness to alter the approach until the desired results are achieved. We'll talk more about the techniques and how to avoid the pitfalls of Extinction and Satiation, but for now, it is just important to have an understanding of what these concepts are.

CHAPTER 8:

Schedules of Reinforcement

As we discussed before, Positive Reinforcement is more than "catch them being good and Reward them" moments. It can be that simple when they are very young, but every child is different and all will require more complex methods over time as they age. Some people give up on Positive Reinforcement after this simplistic method stops working as effectively as it once did. That is really like giving up on reading after only learning the alphabet.

What researchers have found is that not only do the Reinforcers matter, but how often they are given matters a great deal to the success or failure of the Reinforcement. How often can mean, after how many occurrences of the desired Behavior, or after a certain amount of time. A blanket term for this is the Schedule or Schedules of Reinforcement. Reinforcement given after a certain number of occurrences of the desired Behavior is termed ratio and Reinforcement given after a certain amount of time has transpired is termed interval. Reinforcement given after every performance of a Behavior is known as continuous and is what many people associate with Positive Reinforcement.

Continuous reinforcement is simply presenting a Reinforcer after each and every instance of the desired Behavior being performed. There are pros and cons to each type of Schedule, and it is best to use a case by case basis for determining what Schedule will work best in what circumstance with what child and what Reinforcers and Behaviors. If it is a frequent

Pros and Cons of Different Simple Reinforcement Schedules

Ratio Schedules tend to generate a stronger response.

Variable schedules tend to generate a greater resistance to Extinction.

Continuous Reinforcement Schedule:
      Pros: Best for teaching new behaviors. Best schedule for Chaining and Shaping
      Cons: Potentially cost. Effort. Attention required. Highest risk of Satiation.

Fixed Ratio Reinforcement Schedule:
      Pros: High response as reinforcer nears.
      Cons: Response slows after reinforcer. Predictable. Weaker resistance to Extinction.

Variable Ratio Reinforcement Schedule:
      Pros: Highest response rate. Strong resistance to Extinction.
      Cons: Possible disappointment or frustration during stretches without a Reinforcer.

Fixed Interval Reinforcement Schedule:
      Pros: Response rates increase as reinforcer time nears.
      Cons: Can have Extinction levels similar to continuous Reinforcement. Predictable.

Variable Interval Reinforcement Schedule:
      Pros: High response rate. Strong resistance to Extinction.
      Cons: Possible disappointment or frustration during stretches without a Reinforcer.

Behavior, then reinforcing it each time could lead to Satiation, not to mention the potential problems of cost and effort. It is a challenge to be constantly looking out for the Behavior, having Reinforcers with you all the time and reinforcing it. The other problem we discussed in the last chapter is that the Behavior may become extinct quicker than if another

71

Schedule had been used.

Continuous reinforcement is a good choice when a new Behavior must be learned as it helps overcome the discouragement that sometimes accompanies early failures when a new task is being mastered. It can also be helpful when Shaping Behavior, which is something we will talk about in a later chapter. Many people have probably concluded that Positive Reinforcement was too hard because all they knew was Continuous reinforcement. The sad thing

Continuous Reinforcement Schedule

DB ➡ R = 😊 ➡ DB ➡ R = 😊 ➡ DB ➡ R = 😊

DB = Desired Behavior R = Reinforcer   NR = No Reinforcer

is that in many circumstances not only is it the hardest, but it is not even the most effective Schedule.

The next Schedule type would be the Ratio Schedules. Ratios describe the quantity of one thing in relation to the quantity of another thing. In cooking, they will sometimes call for something like three parts water to one part oil. That would be a three to one ratio. So, as you can imagine, a Ratio Schedule will relate the Behavior to the Reinforcer. There are two varieties of Ratio schedule, the first being Fixed Ratio which relates the number of times the Behavior is

'The consequences of behaviors always operate on some sort of schedule, and the schedule can affect the behavior as much as the reinforcement itself.'

performed to how often the Reinforcer is presented. The second form of Ratio Schedule is the Variable Ratio Schedule which still equates the number of performances of the Behavior to the receipt of the Reinforcer but the number necessary changes such that it is, or at least appears to the child, to be random.

The Fixed ratio schedule is really just a variation on the continuous schedule but instead of getting reinforced every time a Behavior is performed, it may be every three times or every five times. The child will quickly come to determine the pattern of how many times the Behavior must be performed until the Reinforcer is presented. Having said that, you can image it has some of the downside of Continuous reinforcement including a tendency to become extinct faster

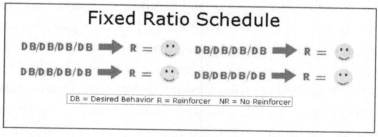

than other Schedules, but because of the intervals of no Reinforcer after one is earned, there is more of a lag in the discovery of a disruption of the Schedule when it stops. An example may be Reinforcing a child clearing the table without being told to do so by presenting the Reinforcer of getting to watch a movie every time they have done it five times. A variation of this is what I like to call all or nothing where they are reinforced for performing the Behavior a set number of times in a row and only if they are consecutive.

The advantages of a Fixed ratio schedule include the fact that because Reinforcers are not given out as often, there is less chance of Satiation or at least it takes longer to set in. Also, because you reinforce less, the cost is potentially less, as well. Cost is always a variable you have control of because you decide the Reinforcers, but you have to choose them from the pool of Reinforcers that will work. The larger your per Reinforcer price, the less Reinforcers you will be able buy and to hand out if you are going to stay on budget. Cost is of course a relative thing as some Reinforcers cost money, some time, and some effort but often they are a combination of two or all of these things to some degree.

The disadvantages of a Fixed Ratio schedule still include potential Satiation although to a lesser degree. Extinction, when stopped is still an issue as I mentioned above but there is a little more Resistance to extinction depending on the ratio of Reinforcers to successfully performed Behaviors. It is not as effective as Continuous reinforcement with teaching new Behaviors. Fixed ratio schedules are rather high maintenance like continuous schedules because even though you are not Reinforcing the Behavior each time, you still constantly need to be paying attention because you have to keep track of what number you are on so you can reinforce the correct instance of the child performing the Behavior.

The other Ratio schedule is the Variable Ratio. Again you don't reinforce the Behavior each time it is performed, but rather you reinforce it randomly. It doesn't have to be truly random, but you want it to at least appear random to the child. You also don't want to wait too long in between Reinforcing the Behavior because even though one of the benefits of a Variable Ratio is Resistance to extinction, you do have to reinforce the Behavior every so often. How old and or mature you child is will help determine how long is the maximum interval between Reinforcers, as well.

One of the best advantages of the Variable Ratio Schedule is that it is easy to maintain and conducive to a busy lifestyle. If you are side tracked and miss the fact that your child just performed the Behavior, you are OK just as long as you don't miss too many. It also has a lower risk of Satiation, as well as being the Schedule most resistant to extinction. This Schedule is weak when it comes to teaching new Behaviors, but other than that, it is very effective. Think of people in casinos who, hour after hour, put coins in the slot machines. Do you think they would be as motivated to play if they just won their coin back every time or if they won three coins every fourth one they put in? Of course not, and even though most people lose money, because the payouts are random, we rationalize that that we could come out ahead, and this mentality seems to be hardwired in our psyches.

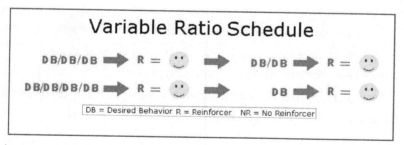

An example would be to have your child wash their hands before dinner. Every so often when they wash their hands without being asked, you could give them dessert that night. They never know which dinner will be the one that could earn them dessert so they have to be prepared for all of them, but you only have to be prepared to let them eat dessert, occasionally. Another example would be something that could potentially happen often and at random times and number of times per day. Let's say you wanted to reinforce your child saying thank you at the appropriate times. This is such a common situation in life that it may be easy to miss them doing it occasionally, and there could be days when they don't have an opportunity, while you are around, to say thank you ,even once. Other days could be one thank you after another. With a Variable Ratio Schedule, you have the flexibility to reinforce whichever scenario.

Next is the Interval schedules which are based on the passage of amounts of time as opposed to the number of times the Behavior was performed. First there is the Fixed Interval schedule where, after a set period of time goes by, the very next instance of the desired Behavior gets reinforced. There is a variation on this schedule similar to the all or nothing option for Fixed Ratio schedules. You can set it up so for a period of time, the child must perform the desired Behavior at each opportunity and then they are reinforced at the end of that period if they didn't miss any chances. The other version of the Interval schedule is the Variable Interval schedule where after a seemingly, to the child, random period of time the next instance of the Behavior is reinforced.

The Fixed Interval schedule has the advantage of being moderately easy to maintain because you don't have to constantly keep track of every possible instance of the desired Behavior. In fact, you can set an alarm on you watch or phone and have it remind you when he next interval has gone by and after it goes off, you just watch for the next instance of the Behavior and reinforce it. The danger of Satiation is no worse than the Fixed ratio schedule, and the rate of Extinction is the same as well and is contingent on how much time goes by before they start figuring out the Reinforcement has stopped. An example would be, if after a four hour interval you reinforce the next instance of your child cleaning up after themselves. The potential problem with a Fixed Interval is that your child can figure out what the interval is and not worry about performing the Behavior until they know it counts toward a Reinforcer, which is especially possible if you are using an alarm as a reminder.

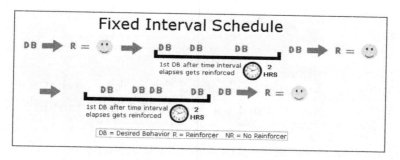

The final schedule is the Variable Interval Schedule. It has the advantage of not having to pay attention at every moment as well as the ability to use reminders such as alarms. It is also resistant to Extinction, and there is less risk of Satiation. While it is not particularly effective when teaching new Behaviors, the other advantages make it appealing. A potential down side to both of the Interval schedules is that you may have to keep changing the intervals because of your schedules and there may be instances of the Behavior that are just so perfect that you want to reinforce them, but if you do then you risk compromising your schedule. An example may be that after a timer goes off, it is set to a new random time each time you set it, and you reinforce the next instance of your child remembering to turn out the light when they leave a room. Having it happen at random intervals makes it almost game like which will keep it more interesting for both you and your child.

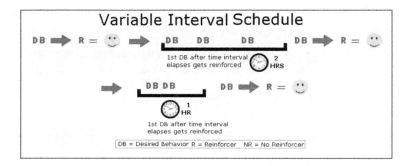

Compound schedules are beyond the realm of what we are trying to cover here, but I thought it was important to know that they exist. A Compound schedule would use combinations of the schedules we discussed or may interchange them so as to keep the Reinforcers coming at different times. For most Caregivers, Compound schedules add a level of complexity, and maintenance and time that would just not justify the added benefits. A simple Schedule should suffice and if none of the variations produce results, then perhaps it's time to pull another parenting tool from the toolbox.

Positive Reinforcement can be very effective for changing Behavior, encouraging the choice of a preferred Behavioral Response and for teaching new Behaviors. For it to be effective however, it must be thought out and planned, by the Caregiver. There is a lot to track and to measure and so written plans and written tracking systems are popular and useful. You will see a variety of charts, checklists and even computer spreadsheets and programs that, will do just that and we will discuss them in a later chapter.

We have learned that what is used as a Reinforcer is important but also when a Reinforcer is presented is vitally important, as well. A continuous Schedule reinforces the Behavior each time it is exhibited, and this can be effective for teaching new Behaviors but is challenging for the Caregiver and can lead to Satiation and Extinction. A Ratio Schedule reinforces Behavior after X number instances of its occurrence while an Interval schedule reinforces the first instance of the Behavior after T period of time. A fixed Schedule reinforces Behavior based on a consistent measure while a Variable Schedule reinforces Behavior based on a changing measure. These combined, form the four base Reinforcement schedules which added to continuous are, Fixed-Interval, Variable Interval, Fixed Ratio and finally Variable Ratio Schedules. Each Schedule has pluses and minuses that must be weighed to find the best fit for the Caregiver and child as well as the most important consideration which is what is effective for this Behavior and this child and this circumstance.

CHAPTER 1 QUIZ ANSWER

2) Maria's Mom wanted her to do her chores after school. To motivate Maria, her Mom made her an Ice cream sundae right when she got home from school. She did this every day for 2 weeks and not only did Maria gain weight, she did her chores on 2 more days than she did on the two week period prior to the daily Reward.

Is this an example of positive reinforcement? (no not tied to performing behavior)

The answer was no.

Many of you said yes because Maria was getting a Reward and it was every day. The problem was that the Reward was not tied to the behavior even though it was on a regular schedule. The fact that the behavior increased was incidental as she was given the treat on days that she ended up not doing her chores as well.

If the ice cream were given after the chores were complete and not given when chores not done AND the frequency of the chores being done increased, then it would have been Positive Reinforcement.

CHAPTER 9:

Punishment, Shaping and Chaining

Punishment

We will first examine Punishment. Punishment almost feels like a taboo subject in this day and age and conjures up an image of spanking a child. Punishment is not some evil torture tactic our grandparents used to use shame and regret of the family. It is rare, if ever, that you hear the words Punishment and Positive Reinforcement in the same sentence, let alone the same book. Punishment is just another Caregiver tool and is not the opposite of Positive Reinforcement and is not mutually exclusive to Positive Reinforcement.

Let's start by saying that this book is not about Punishment, but it is important to discuss its relationship with Positive Reinforcement in a clinical, technical way, from an emotional viewpoint, as well as a seeing it as a generational social paradigm shift. We'll get into the technical side in a moment but first let's look at the social aspects and connotations. Let's face it, corporal Punishment, spanking etc., was once a key component to child rearing. Read novels from times past and you'll quickly see that children were treated, by today's standards, quite harshly up until relatively recently.

CHAPTER 1 QUIZ ANSWER

5) Coach Kevin, from the team above, had to quit and so Coach Sara took his place. She wasn't sure his method was working so instead of telling each player something positive every time before they batted, she decided to encourage them if only if they did not get a hit when they returned to the dugout. Sure enough, over the course of the next two games the kids got more hits.

Is this an example of positive reinforcement?

The answer was no.

Many of you said yes because the talk was directed at specific performance and led to increased results. The problem is, getting hits was not the behavior being addressed, NOT getting a hit was what was being addressed. As the behavior actually decreased we must conclude that what was being done was positive punishment.

Many of you, like me, were spanked as children, and many of you, like me, at some point spanked your child. I don't think it was right to do as my child was not defiant, but rather, he has Asperger Syndrome (which in my defense, I didn't know at the time) and it proved ineffective. I would certainly not judge someone who also tried this tool in the parenting toolbox. I am not a degreed professional and this book is not about spanking and whether it's right or wrong, but I can only say from my personal experience that it was not effective for my child, and it did not do my psyche very much good as a Parent. If you spank your child, all I have to say is that different forms of Operant condoning, including both Punishment and Reinforcement, are not mutually exclusive. It is not an either or choice, but you may find one is more effective than the other for a given child, in a given circumstance, for a given Behavior.

I have read a lot about Positive Reinforcement over the years, and I will be the first to point out that a good deal of it discusses Positive Reinforcement as an alternative to Punishment. You will have to decide that for yourself. They act like if you are to properly use Positive Reinforcement you can never ground a child or use a time out or take away a privilege or toy. The attitude is that you should ignore all the "bad" Behaviors and find a way to Reward their "good" counterparts. While I agree with looking there first, I don't think it is always practical, and I don't think Positive Reinforcement is always the best parenting tool for a given problem. Tell the Parent of a 14 year old who snuck out and got drunk or the Parent of a four year old who defiantly hits his Mom in the face with a toy that Punishment should never be used and unwanted Behavior just ignored.

Behavior Goals
Reinforcement = To Strengthen a Behavioral
Punishment = To Weaken a Behavior

Consequence Actions of Punishment
Positive = Adding an Aversive Stimulus
Negative = Subtracting an Appetitive Stimulus

Stimuli
"Appetitive stimulus = a pleasant outcome
Aversive stimulus = an unpleasant outcome" z065

For me, I am a pragmatist and look for what is effective rather than being tied to dogma. Again, I am not a professional Therapist, so keep in mind these are the musings of an experienced Parent added in with materials from professionals about this subject matter, designed to give the reader a better understanding of Positive Reinforcement. I will get off my soapbox for now and we will take a look at Punishment from a more technical viewpoint.

Punishment is the weakening of a Behavior as opposed to Reinforcement being the strengthening of a Behavior. So we want to Reinforce desired Behaviors while punishing unwanted Behaviors. Punishment, like Reinforcement, comes in two varieties, Positive and Negative. Like Reinforcement, Positive means to add a Stimulus while negative means to take away a Stimulus and neither has the good or bad connotations we have already covered at length with Reinforcement. The one important ingredient, no matter what the Punishment, is that it must then lead to a decrease in the

Working Definitions

Positive Punishment for Children: The adding of a result or consequence that the child finds unpleasant, dependent on the occurrence of a certain behavior or response by the child, which results in a decrease in the likelihood of that behavior or response in the child, because of the added result or consequence.

Negative Punishment for Children: The removal of a result or consequence that the child finds pleasant, dependent on the occurrence of a certain behavior or response by the child, which results in a decrease in the likelihood of that behavior or response in the child, because of the removed result or consequence.

target Behavior just as Reinforcement must result in an increase in the Behavior or it's not Punishment in the former, or Reinforcement in the latter.

If I were to say "Negative Punishment", I bet thoughts of spanking, yelling or some sort of thing like that pops into your head. If I were to say Positive Punishment I'm sure that just strikes the ears wrong like "little giants" or "green orange". We have to toss these notions out and drill in our definitions again. Positive Punishment adds an Aversive stimulus while Negative Punishment takes away an Appetitive stimulus.

So Positive Punishment would cover such tactics as spanking, yelling, having to pull weeds, cleaning desks after school, etc. Negative Punishment would include grounding or restriction, loss of certain privileges, time out, etc. Time outs could be argued don't belong here because it would depend on the context as time outs in many forms are supposed to be a cooling off period and not a Punishment, but I don't want to digress into the finer distinctions of time out techniques.

What can be difficult, is determining what category a consequence falls into. For instance, classify the following:

Your child has forgotten to do her chores again. You make her go to bed early.

A) This is Positive Punishment because you are adding 30 minutes to the time she must lay in bed awake.

B) This is Negative Punishment because you are taking 30 minutes of time should could be having fun away from her.

A case could be made for both but in an instance where it is too close to call, the Caregiver who ultimately knows the child best could determine which applies more to this child.

Beyond that, does it really matter? We are talking about two types of Punishment and no matter whether it is Positive or Negative, at the end of the day, they are implemented with the goal of weakening the Behavior.

Next, we will look at Shaping and Chaining. These are more advanced methods of implementing Operant Conditioning that may involve Reinforcement or Punishment. We will try to focus more in their use with Positive Reinforcement, but you should know that the four main types of Operant Conditioning can be used in Shaping and Chaining.

Shaping

Shaping and Chaining are two techniques for teaching more complex Behaviors. As a new Behavior is generally involved, a Continuous reinforcement schedule is used or actually an approximation of one as we will see. First let's discuss Shaping. I have often heard Shaping described as a game of hot and cold. You know that game we played as kids where you are trying to direct someone to a location or thing and as they take a step closer to it you say "getting warmer" and when they take a step away from it you would say "colder". Waiting for someone to walk right up to the location or thing that is "it" would take a frustratingly long time whereas reinforcing them with each little progress toward the ultimate goal works pretty efficiently. That in essence is Shaping.

A more practical example of Shaping would be teaching a child to play a sport. I'm going to use baseball as I have first-hand experience having played as a child and with my son playing but the principal is the same with any sport or really any complex activity. You can show a child a game of baseball being played and then hand them a glove and tell them to go play, but unless somehow magically gifted, that child would be destined to fail. Go to a child's baseball practice and you will see that the complex activity we know as a baseball game is a set of complex Behaviors in Response varied but finite stimuli. These complex Behaviors are shaped starting on day one where they hand the children a ball and tell them to grab their gloves. They show the kids the basics of throwing and catching and then pair them up just a short distance in front of each other and have them toss the ball back and forth. The coaches verbally reinforce successful Behaviors such as a mechanically correct throw or getting a glove in front of the ball, regardless of whether they caught it or not. Go back six weeks later and there is no praise for getting the glove in front of the ball as that is now expected, the praise is for a difficult catch or long throw.

The same goes with batting. Children who have never played before don't just pick up a bat and start hitting home runs. They are shown fundamentals and praised for performing the fundamentals until they become ingrained and the more complex component of the Behavior is then taught and praised, all built on the simpler approximations of the more complex Behavior that was taught, performed, reinforced and mastered as a step toward learning the more complex Behavior of batting. On day one, just holding the bat correctly was reinforced and after weeks of training, practice, and Reinforcement the complex Behavior of getting a hit in a game is learned, and the act is reinforced to an even greater degree as the crowd cheers and no longer does each progressive step need to be reinforced.

Shaping can at times be guided by Extinction Bursts. As Shaping is used in teaching new Behaviors, it is mostly reinforced using a Continuous reinforcement schedule. As we learned previously, a downside of using a Continuous reinforcement schedule that Extinction can happen quickly when Reinforcement is stopped. We also learned that in the initial phases of Extinction, a child may try variations on their previous Behavior in order to try get the Reinforcer to be presented again. In Shaping, this experimentation phase gets the child to progress in different directions, speaking figuratively but it could be literally as well. Once the child starts to progress closer toward the final desired Behavior they are reinforced again, and this continues until the child is able to perform it.

A last example may be having a child clean their room. The task may be overwhelming but picking up just the red toys and putting them away today and maybe just dirty clothes the next day etc. will make it more manageable. Having the child focus on just the small task and the Reinforcer they will earn will minimize the enormity of the task to the child. Like the old saying, that asks how you eat an elephant ...one bite at a time. At some point, the child could be just reinforced for cleaning their room as they built up their ability to handle a larger and larger cleaning task until they are able to handle the whole room at one time.

Using Shaping to mold a great room cleaner
GOAL: CLEAN ROOM
1) Messy Room

2) Remove the 3 things that are not balls but go through the air
One small Reinforcer when done

3) Put away things without wheels that have red in them
One small Reinforcer when done

4) Put away all the toys with wheels

One small Reinforcer when done

5) Put away the sports equipment

One large Reinforcer when done

Celebrate the larger task
and how the simple little
jobs took care of the big
job that seemed so hard.

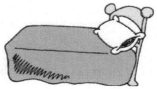

Chaining

Chaining, like Shaping, is useful for teaching new and complex Behaviors. A Continuous reinforcement schedule works best as that is the Schedule most conducive to learning new Behaviors. While Shaping is like the kids game hot or cold, Chaining is more like the kids game Mousetrap(TM) where you have to put the pieces together one step at a time in the exact order or it won't work. At the end of the game, the whole contraption works because the players successfully assembled it in order.

Chaining is essentially breaking down a complex Behavior into a series of 1-2-3, steps where each leads to the next. An example for visualization purposes is making a cake. First you do this and then that, and they must be done in sequence or you don't end up with a cake. A practical example might be having to learn to recite the Gettysburg Address for Social Studies class. It could be broken down into one or two sentences that can be learned one at a time with a Reinforcer set up for once each successive step is learned. So after a few days, the opening line is memorized. Next the child learns to

CHAINING

Four score and seven years ago **═ Reinforcer!**
THEN
Four score and seven years ago **═ Reinforcer!**
our fathers brought forth
THEN
Four score and seven years ago
our fathers brought forth **═ Reinforcer!**
on this continent a new nation,

add the second line and a Reinforcer is provided once the first two lines, steps 1 and 2, can be recited at one siting. The Reinforcers could be identical, or perhaps they could get more elaborate with each step, but the point is, the large task is broken down into smaller steps and each sequential step is reinforced.

Chaining is very useful for more complex Behaviors, with complex being a relative term based on how the child relates to the Behavior at hand. Tying a shoe can be complex to a six year old while easy for a teenager. Overwhelming can be

94

substituted for complex in the first sentence as washing a load of clothes can be overwhelming for one child but a piece of cake for another child of the same age. Almost any larger Behavior can be broken down into tasks and reinforced, if the tasks are sequential in nature then we are talking about Chaining. For instance if it is essential or even preferential for step two to be performed after step 1 and before step 3 then it is Chaining.

Backwards Chaining is, as you may guess, the exact opposite in that you teach the end result then reinforce each successive step going backwards, Reinforcing each one until you get back to the very first step. Whether you would use forward or backward Chaining, would depend on the type of Behavior you are trying to teach. Certain Behaviors would not be conducive to Backwards Chaining like the example of learning a speech since if you could start at learning the whole speech you wouldn't need to learn the individual lines afterward. Some Behaviors may benefit from this technique. One example may be learning to put together a tent. To teach a child to do this, it may help to start with the finished product and teach the steps leading up to that in reverse order so when they go to put it together they can visualize what the completion of that step looks like before it is done.

Both Shaping and Chaining are methods of teaching new Behaviors and not really meant for the maintenance of known or existing Behaviors. The goal of each is to reinforce the parts until finally just the complex Behavior itself can be reinforced. That is not to say that it cannot be applied to old or known Behaviors, for instance to use a previous example, a child who has been cleaning their own room for years could be reinforced with Shaping. Essentially, although an old Behavior, cleaning their room, is addressed, the technique is really what is being taught and reinforced. The breaking down of the large task is a new Behavior, and in the end, the room cleaning Behavior is now arrived at by a new method.

In conclusion, Chaining is really just a specific kind of Shaping. More complex Behaviors can be taught by breaking them down into their component parts for Shaping, or steps in Chaining, and then each component, or step, is reinforced until the child has learned to do the complex Behavior. These techniques lend themselves to teaching new Behaviors or new ways of doing complex Behaviors that the child is struggling with. The Behaviors that can be taught to a child using these methods is relative to the individual child as different children at different ages find Behaviors to be more or less complex and more or less overwhelming.

CHAPTER 10:

Positive Reinforcement Systems

The vast majority of you probably fall into one of two groups at this point, those who have never heard of the term Token Economy and those who are asking how the heck we made it all the way to chapter ten before discussing them. A Token Economy is a system where Tokens such as points, tickets, chips or some other secondary or Generalized Reinforcer are used as Reinforcers for performing desired Behaviors and the Tokens can be accumulated and later redeemed for a Primary Reinforcer or a choice of Primary Reinforcers for a predetermined number of Tokens. Token Economies are usually used in conjunction with Positive Reinforcement but could be used with other Operant conditioners. For instance, Negative Reinforcement by having the Primary Reinforcer be an Aversive stimulus that would be removed when enough Tokens are earned and Negative Punishment where the child loses Tokens for misbehavior, or in Positive Punishment with something like a three strikes and you're out system.

A Token Economy is simply a fancy way of saying a system where a symbol or item is assigned a value within the system itself, even if worthless outside the system. Tokens themselves can be anything that works for you but some examples would be tickets, marbles, plastic coins, play money, cards, points, stickers, etc. Usually the Tokens can be redeemed for tangible items, but it doesn't have to be a thing at all but can be whatever type of Reinforcer you want to include. The child must know what the Reinforcers are, or at least, have some sort of idea what they may be so that the Tokens can be valued by the child. For example, a teacher may hand out poker chips for good Behavior that can be used as a currency in a "goodie store" filled with party favor type toys and gadgets.

Ticket Chart

The money system of the world is nothing more than a Token Economy. Our Tokens are the special pieces of paper and coins designated with vales assigned to them. The paper and coins are essentially worthless outside of this system, which you can imagine, when you think of what a five dollar bill would be worth to a group of people stranded on an island with little chance of being rescued. These Tokens can be redeemed anywhere within the system for items. People are reinforced to show up at businesses day after day and perform specific tasks and then take the Tokens they earn and exchange them for goods and services. This all works, of course, because we know the value of the Tokens based on what we know we can get with them, which is why it's important for your child to know what his or her Tokens will be able to get for them.

Token Economies are very popular and very effective because they solve some basic problems of implementing Positive Reinforcement. The first problem is that of the Reinforcer itself. If you plan on using a Tangible Reinforcer, then you are going to end up with a house full of party favor type trinkets or an empty bank account from cleaning out the local  toy store. The second problem has to do with the frequency of Reinforcers because if the Tangible Reinforcer is costly, it cannot be given out very often and to make the Reinforcement work then Reinforcers must be given out with some degree of regularity no matter what Reinforcement Schedule you are on. The third problem is the practical delivery and timing of the Reinforcers. Tokens may be easily carried around and given right at the time of the target Behavior, no matter what the setting or location is.

Let's get back to the first problem of the Reinforcer itself. Even when dealing with small children, giving out stickers or trinket toys will get old for them, and they will hit a point of Satiety and the Reinforcer will no longer be effective, or at least not as effective, in reinforcing the target Behavior. The flip side is to give larger or more valuable Reinforcers, but this tends to translate into higher costs to the Caregiver and frankly the Reinforcer's monetary value will quickly outstrip the Behaviors value to the Caregiver. Token Economies bridge the gap by allowing for the excitement and motivation of larger Reinforcers while also allowing the lower cost and frequent Reinforcement of the smaller Reinforcers.

The second problem had to do with the frequency of the Reinforcer. We're back to giving trinkets frequently and leading to Satiety or larger Reinforcers leading to spoiled children and broke Caregivers. The alternative is to give larger Reinforcers but less frequently. No matter what Schedule of Reinforcement you are using, it is important to give relatively regular Reinforcers. If you have ever played the slot machines, you will see this in action as occasionally the player will just win back their coin or maybe just a couple of coins. If people only won something when they hit the big prize, and didn't have the frequent little Reinforcement, they would get discouraged and quit playing fairly quickly.

The third problem was the practical delivery and timing of the Reinforcers. You ideally want to deliver the Reinforcer in the moment of the Behavior or shortly thereafter. If the Reinforcer is a toy truck, it may not be practical to present it if you are away from home like in the grocery store. Caregivers can easily carry around a few Tokens so that they may be given where they are and always handy at the time the desired Behavior is being performed.

There is another thing that is really more of an added benefit, and that is the fact that Tokens are Generalized Reinforcers, which we discussed back in the chapter on Reinforcers. Basically they are associated with a number of Reinforcers which can be changed out, added to or subtracted from easily, without effecting the Tokens, Token value or the system itself. You can also use the same Token Reward system with more than one Behavior, so if you are trying to reinforce two or three Behaviors, then you can use Tokens for all three instead of coming up with two or three different Reinforcers and tracking progress toward each. Even if the Behaviors have differing levels of difficulty, you can adjust for this by setting the number of Tokens the child earns for the Behavior exhibited.

For example, let's say you are using Positive Reinforcement to encourage your son to keep his elbows off the table during dinner and to complete his homework by a certain time. The homework may be a much more difficult Behavior for your child, so the successful completion may be worth three Tokens while keeping his elbows off the table may only be worth one.

Setting up a Token Economy can be as straight forward or as complicated as you like. When my kids were younger, I personally used a simple piece of paper with a picture of the goal Reinforcer at the top and a grid, with x number squares that had to be filled with stickers before the Reinforcer was earned. I always like to buy stickers with a theme my sons liked and would give them the sticker to place on the chart themselves, providing an added bonus feeling of accomplishment. They can get a lot more complicated if you like, as well. You can use a point system and have a catalog of choices and there are even web sites and software packages out there that help you do that.

For some of you, Token Economies may seem like a totally new or foreign concept, but I'm here to tell you that at least most, if not all of you, have been a participant in at least one besides our monetary economy. Many of you were probably part of one in school as many teachers across the world for decades have but utilizing Token Economies in the classroom to help learning and control Behavior but I'm not talking about that either. I bet most of you have received some frequent-flier miles from an airline or points on a credit card redeemable for merchandise, or how about those tickets you win playing skeet ball that you redeem for toys at a booth, or how about a card that gets check marks on a card at a sub shop good for a free sandwich after so many? Any of these sound familiar.

Token Economies are all around us as adults and they have been proven very successful in modifying Behavior or why else would so many huge companies be running and expanding them. I should know, for many years I designed online incentive programs for fortune 500 clients working for a leading incentive company. In fact, my primary work was for my firm's largest client, which is currently one of Forbes 10 largest companies in America. Token Economies work very well on molding adult Behavior, and there is no reason why we as Parents should not also be able to employ this very successful tool as well.

Tokens are Secondary Reinforcers while the things they are redeemed for are Primary Reinforcers. I mentioned some of the benefits of a Token Economy above, as they solve several problems as well as allow for flexibility. They also automate some of the tasks of parenting so you don't have to think so much about what needs to be done, or Rewards, or Punishments, or who needs to be doing what. The system tends to spell a lot of that out and the children know what it all is and this leaves you time to think and spend resources on more important parenting tasks like instilling values, teaching and loving. Have you ever been so flustered and overwhelmed as a Parent that when your child did something you disapproved of you just couldn't even function and spat out some gibberish that you look back on and wondered what the heck you were saying? Token Economies help clear the plate, so you don't have to get to that place.

As I have pointed out several times, I am not a degreed therapist or psychology professional, but besides being an incentives expert, I have two boys, one of which has Asperger Syndrome. Speaking from my experiences, I have found that Token Economies are good at helping children become introduced to the concept of goal setting, and then also Reinforcing that concept by allowing them to pick their goal time frame and trying very hard to earn the Tokens they need to achieve their goal. There is also a certain amount of delayed gratification learned as they have to work at their Behaviors now, to earn Tokens for the ultimate Reinforcer they will receive later. I always like to put a mix of lower and greater value items in my sons' "catalogs" of Reinforcers they can redeem Tokens for, so that in order to get the bigger items, they need to resist the quick easy lower value ones, and again, delay gratification.

In this chapter, we learned that Token Economies are very popular and very effective because they solve some basic problems of implementing Positive Reinforcement. Because they allow a Caregiver to break the value of a larger Reinforcer into smaller valued Tokens, they reduce the cost of Positive Reinforcement and allow for Reinforcers to be delivered at the time of the Behavior, wherever the child is, and allows the Caregiver to have a supply of Tokens with them most of the time. Because larger Reinforcers can be delivered, the problem of Satiety is greatly reduced, and because Tokens are Generalized Reinforcers, multiple Behaviors can be addressed with the same system. Finally, Token Economies automate some parenting tasks as well as teach goal setting and delayed gratification.

CHAPTER 11:

Positive Reinforcement Techniques

Here, is where we get into the practical nuts and bolts of how to implement Positive Reinforcement. If you have never done this before, it can be a little scary or overwhelming as a Caregiver. My advice is to start small and give both yourself and your child an opportunity to learn how it works and learn the specific things that do work and don't work for your specific circumstances. There are so many variables such as age, and medical and/or psychological issues, your relationship with your child, how much or what times you see your child, whether they are in school and whether or not you work, and on and on.

One thing we haven't talked about is getting the other Caregivers on board with the program. Getting on the same page as your spouse, or a relative that watches your child, or whoever is important in the care of your child, but how you do that is a topic for another book. Suffice to say, that if the Caregivers are not in agreement, whatever you do will not be as effective as it could be.

One last consideration is siblings. Speaking from personal experience, I felt it was important to have both my boys on a program, so neither one felt left out. You know your children best, but even if there is one child who needs this more than the other, it certainly won't hurt the one, or ones, who need it less. The main consideration I feel you need to address is that of sibling rivalry and competition. Some children thrive under the same rules and structure, and benefit from each other's support and success. Then there are my kids, who made it the kind of competition where tears would be shed if one brother earned a Reinforcer while the other still hadn't. My solution was to come up with two simple but totally different systems for each boy so they were apples and oranges and the competition was minimalized. Again, you know what's best for your children.

I will now go into detail with each step.

1. Create a list of Behaviors to add, stop or change

Basic Steps of a Positive Reinforcement Program

1) Create a list of behaviors to add, stop or change

2) Rank these behaviors by importance to you and by difficulty for your child to change, add or stop

3) Brainstorm a list of possible reinforcers

4) Choose a single behavior and a motivating reinforcer

5) Choose your system and set it up system (chart, picture, etc)

6) Sit down with your child and explain

7) Coach your child for first couple reinforcers and then start to back off

8) Deliver reinforcer as appropriate

9) Give feedback!

10) Track and measure effectiveness

11) Evaluate and tweak if necessary

12) Repeat, add, or replace new target behavior

This is a brainstorming session. You may be clear on exactly what you want to work on here, but this is a useful exercise, just listing all the Behaviors that come to mind, even if you don't ultimately address them all with Positive Reinforcement. Sometimes we get so fixated on one Behavior that particularly bugs us that we don't see that it is a symptom of a larger  problem. For example, let's say your mornings are hectic because your child is hard to get going in the morning, and it's a struggle and you want to address that. Maybe they are having a hard time focusing on their homework in the afternoon, as well. Listing these out could lead you to ask the question, is my child getting enough sleep? Maybe the real Behavior to address is getting to bed on time at night.

2. Rank these Behaviors by importance to you and by difficulty for your child to change, add or stop

The first thing you must do is try and turn the desired  Behavior change into an action or Behavior you would want to see. We tend to see these Behaviors in their terms we don't like. For instance, we may say we want Sally to stop lying or Juan to stop hitting his brother. We could also say we want Sally to tell the truth and Juan to get along with his brother. It is very hard to talk about this without using the terms positive and negative, but I don't want to create any confusion. We want to list the Behaviors in terms we want our children to move toward instead of terms they should move away from. If you cannot identify that

112

"moving towards" Behavior then perhaps another method, such as Punishment, should be examined.

Once you have identified and modified your list, you need to rank them in order of importance to you of them changing. You should know your priorities here. Next, copy the list and this time, rank it in terms of difficulty for your child. Finally, ask yourself if the Behavior you want to address is appropriate for Positive Reinforcement or is there another tool in the parenting toolbox that may be more useful to try first.

3. Brainstorm a list of possible Reinforcers

Next, you should create a list of Reinforcers that your child would like. Think beyond Tangible Reinforcers  by including the other types we discussed in Chapter 6. These include Activity, Sensory and Social. Don't be afraid to elicit your child's help with this task. Not many kids have a problem putting together a birthday list, so this should be easy. You can also get this information by asking them, "What is your favorite...". You can complete that sentence with food, sound, TV show, game, thing you like to do with me, etc. Compile your list and add a price tag, if any, and a time value for how much time you will need to invest.

4. Choose a single Behavior and a motivating Reinforcer

The assumption here is that Positive Reinforcement is new to either you or your child or both of you. If this is your first time, don't pick the most challenging Behavior to get your feet wet with. Make sure you have a crystal clear picture in your head of what you are looking for and write it down. It is essential to write it down so you and your child can refer to it and both of you know what a success looks like. Put down what you don't want, as well, if you think that will help clarify the goal, but try and keep it as upbeat and focused on the desired outcome as possible.

Try and pick a motivating Reinforcer but also one that on par with the difficulty of the Behavioral change. Now is the time to discuss the Reinforcer with your child to make sure it is properly motivating to them and not just something you think should be motivating to them. You may think comic books are stupid and baseball cards cool, but it is not you who is being asked to change their Behavior and work hard towards a goal. The Reinforcer must be something you child likes, wants, cannot easily get elsewhere and is motivated by.

5. Choose your system and set it up system

This could be as easy as, "do this and earn that" or it can be an elaborate Token Economy. If you are new to all this, I would recommend keeping it simple with small Reinforcers given directly as a Reinforcer for the Behavior. If you are picking a larger Reinforcer, then I recommend a simple chart with a number of squares that need to be checked or have a sticker placed on them, to earn the Reinforcer. But, we are getting ahead of ourselves here a bit.

Let's first look at a Schedule of Reinforcement. If this is a new Behavior then you may need to start out with Continuous reinforcement and then move onto a different Schedule. The different Schedules can be confusing just to tell apart and don't easily lend themselves to being self-evident as which one you should choose. There are some basic considerations like how many opportunities for Reinforcement will you have per day. Also, keep in mind whether or not you will be able to keep track of how many times a Behavior has occurred since the last time you reinforced it.

You have the Ratio schedules that reinforce based on the number of times the Behavior has been exhibited since it was last reinforced. The  crucial thing here is you have to keep track, which can be difficult if you have a life. Of course if you go with the Variable Ratio you could reinforce it when you see it and think of it making sure you don't reinforce it every time. For Behaviors that happen a lot, this was always the method that worked best for me. The good news is not only is it easier for the Caregiver, since you don't have to be a perfect tracker, but it is probably the most effective Schedule for getting your child to exhibit the desired Behavior. This seems like a real win-win.

We also have the Interval schedules which may work better for you or your situation. There is the fixed interval which reinforces the first time the Behavior is done after a set period of time has passed since the last Reinforcer was given, and the variable interval that randomizes the amount of time instead of having a set time. These could be very practical if you paired them with an alarm on your phone or perhaps a calendar that sends texts to your phone as reminders. This has the advantage of being not only an indicator of the interval passing, but a reminder in general so we don't forget during the course of our busy days. A fixed interval Reinforcement that worked well for me was the Reinforcement chart review at the end of the day, where we went to the chart and we reviewed how they did for the day, and stickers were earned that they then put on their progress chart toward the Reinforcer they were working towards.

6. Sit down with your child and explain

Once you have your program planned out it's time to sit down with your child and explain it. Remember that Positive Reinforcement is about changing Behavior, not about changing your child. When discussing it with them, discuss it in terms of the Behaviors that will be addressed. For instance you wouldn't tell little Mary that she is mean or not nice so you are going to work on her being nice. Hitting, or not getting along, is the issue you are going to be working on and getting along and not hitting, will earn the Reinforcer.

You have to commit to following through with the program 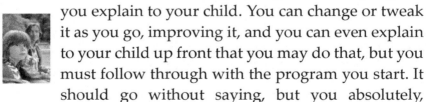 you explain to your child. You can change or tweak it as you go, improving it, and you can even explain to your child up front that you may do that, but you must follow through with the program you start. It should go without saying, but you absolutely, positively must go through with the Reinforcer after they

116

have performed the Behavior to earn it. You can do damage beyond the program and the target Behavior if you go back on your word as you can damage the trust and belief they have in you. But, if you we're the kind of Caregiver who didn't already know that, then you wouldn't have gotten this book, let alone read this far.

7. Coach your child for the first couple Reinforcers and then start to back off

Remember to reinforce more at first until your child gets the hang of what's going on as this may be totally new to them and if not the whole concept of Positive Reinforcement, then at least the idea of doing this new or different Behavior. You may need to reinforce movement toward the new Behavior until they get the hang of it or develop the skills needed to correctly exhibit the new Behavior. Help and coach your child at the start as changing Behavior is hard. Even if the thing you are asking them to do is easy, in your perspective, remembering to think about it can be a challenge until old Behaviors are broken and new ones take their place. They say old habits are hard to break and what are habits but just entrenched Behavior patterns. Empathize with your children and don't be afraid to share stories of your own struggles with Behavior change, it will bond you.

8. Deliver Reinforcer as appropriate

The goal is to deliver the Reinforcer in the moment of the  Behavior, so the child can make that link and create that good feeling to doing this new Behavior. The longer you wait, from the time of the Behavior, to the time of the Reinforcer, the less effective it will be. There will be times and/or Behaviors that don't lend themselves to that instant Reinforcement, that's alright. One thing that I did was to review what they did detail, or better yet, have them go into detail talking about the Behavior and what they did so as to relive the moment and then give them the Reinforcer.

You may be using Social Reinforcers for your program. If you are not it may be a good idea to pair Social Reinforcers with whatever else you are doing because it not only does it increase the number of Reinforcers, it gives an opportunity for feedback, which we will discuss next.

9. Give feedback!

Almost everything I ever read about Positive Reinforcement stops after the Reinforcer is delivered as if you are done at that point. I think this is a huge mistake and may come out the animal training roots of these concepts. You have a child who just did the Behavior you have wanted and feeling proud and good about themselves and good about you. You certainly have their attention as you are about to give them a Reinforcer and they know it. Use this rare gift of undivided attention to talk about why you want them to do this Behavior and what it will mean for their lives and why eventually they will do the Behavior and feel good about it for those reasons.

118

A lot of criticism, which we will address later in the book, stems from the fact that when the Reinforcer stops, so does the Behavior and that the child should do the Behavior because of internal motivations and not external motivations. I agree that if you stop at step 8, then this is a valid criticism. I hated reading as a child and didn't really discover its joys until college. If I had been positively reinforced at an earlier age, I not only would have gotten past the block I had, my Caregiver could have discussed the book and the joys and all the great things about reading, including stories of their own experience. I might have resisted, at first, and maybe only did it for the Reinforcer, but I would have built a new habit, developed the skills and muscles, if you will, and needed for reading. I could not get excited about the new worlds that reading presents because I wasn't reading to get to those new worlds. Positive Reinforcement is a means and not an ends.

Saying things like "way to go" and good job is OK, but they don't become effective until you tie them to something concrete and specific. If Johnny says thank you, which was the desired Behavior, and you say "good job", that doesn't really tell him much and gets lost with the thousands of other "good jobs" he hears. Better is to say, "Good job remembering to say thank you. You let that other boy know that you appreciated getting your ball back and that you noticed that he made the effort to bring it to you when he didn't have to. Doesn't that make you feel good letting him know all that with just two words?" Remember, with praise, more is not necessarily better if it is empty or generalized but more specific and detailed is always more effective.

10. Track and measure effectiveness

This is one of the most difficult parts of a Positive Reinforcement program. We all lead busy lives, and it is not always easy to remember how many times you saw your child do the new Behavior, especially if you are on a Schedule other than Continuous reinforcement. Try to work it into the systems you already have in place in your life. If you

	A	B
	Date	Clean Room
1	1-Jan	yes
2	2-Jan	yes
3	3-Jan	no
4	4-Jan	yes
5	5-Jan	yes
6	6-Jan	yes
7	7-Jan	yes
8	8-Jan	yes
9	9-Jan	yes
10	10-Jan	no
11	11-Jan	yes

have paper lists, box off a corner of them for keeping track of Behavior. If you are a computer person, then keep a list or spreadsheet on your computer. Most of us have our phones with us at all times so send yourself a voice mail, email or text to keep track. It doesn't have to be an elaborate thing, just keep tabs of how many times they do it per day or how many times they do vs. how many opportunities they had to do it, whatever. The important thing is you want to see if there is an increase in the desired Behavior.

Don't get too hung up in the numbers. You definitely want to see an improvement in the number of times a Behavior occurs, but there are other intangibles, such as, are they trying and maybe not succeeding quite yet? This could lead to a coaching or teaching opportunity. Maybe they do it slightly more but also their attitude about doing it is positive, where they maybe would do it before but it was a struggle or a hassle. Measure whatever is important to you and if that is getting better, then it is working. If you spelled out the desired

Behavior properly in step 4, then it should be easy to measure the success, or failure to achieve success, of the program.

11. Evaluate and tweak if necessary

You have to track and evaluate to determine if your program is effective. Is the Reinforcer motivating them? Are you seeing more of the desired Behavior? Is your child motivated by the program? If the answer is no, or I don't know to any of these questions, then you need to tweak the program. This can be increasing the frequency of the Reinforcers, changing the Schedule, changing the Reinforcer or whatever you think will help make it better. Don't be afraid to get your child's input. Maybe you are offering a big Saturday fishing trip and your child didn't want to hurt your feelings but hates the idea of fishing.

Just because it's working, doesn't mean you don't have to tweak it occasionally, as well. In fact, that may be the time to start spacing out the Reinforcers a little bit. If things are going really well and there is another Behavior you would like to reinforce, it may be a good time to try that, as well. You may be just happy that things are going well and want to leave them alone. If you are comfortable with that, then that is fine too just don't rest on your laurels when it comes to tracking

> **'Positive Reinforcement is a means and not an ends'**

because it may be working great now but Satiation, or something else, may be right around the corner.

12. Repeat, add, or replace new target Behavior

OK, so the desired Behavior change has been accomplished and you have weaned them off of the Reinforcers, being careful to look for signs of Extinction. Now what? If there is another Behavior you would like to see changed, then start at step 1 with that Behavior. If you are working towards a more complex Behavior by Chaining them introduce the next step.

We have learned the steps to assembling a Positive Reinforcement program. There will be unforeseen bumps and issues along the way that have not been accounted for here, but such is life. You have a framework with which to build your program and you will overcome the challenges and figure out what works best for your child and you as you go. As long as the intentions, motivations, attitude and spirit of the program are good, then I think even an unsuccessful attempt is far better than no attempt. Even if no Behavior change was accomplished at all, it shows your child that you care about them and love them enough to try. If at first you don't succeed then try, try again and if ultimately Positive Reinforcement is not for you, fortunately there are other tools in the parenting toolbox.

CHAPTER 12:

Positive Reinforcement in a Group Setting

The book is primarily aimed at Positive Reinforcement on a  more individualized level, but I would be remiss if I didn't discuss it in a group setting, where it can work wonders, as well. From teachers in classrooms, to coaches of sport teams, Leaders in activities that range from Scouting, to Church and community based groups, to counselors at camps, to you name it. If you are dealing with a group of kids, Positive Reinforcement programs can be a lifesaver. They provide Behavioral objectives which function as a set of expectations and rules as well as provide structure for the Leader of the group. We will switch to the term Leader, in the group context, taking the place of the Caregiver moniker used at the individualized level.

The same principals apply to group settings as to individual Positive Reinforcement, for the most part. Your program and desired Behaviors must be clearly spelled out. This of course is even more important as you add additional children because you need to make sure each and every child knows what is expected, what is being reinforced and how. Misunderstandings can destroy the program. I would recommend increasing the simplicity as the group size increases. If you can't increase the simplicity, at least decrease the complexity. This sounds contradictory but, for example, a program can have lots of rules that are individually very simple and can't be reduced to a simpler state, but because there are so many of them the program itself is complex.

You also have the group dynamic to account for, which can help or hurt you depending on how well you understand the principals of group dynamics and how well you understand your specific group. Whole books are spent discussing group theory, so you can delve into that more with one of those. What you don't want to do is turn kids against each other or put a spotlight on any single kid's or group of kids' weaknesses. You also don't want your system of Positive Reinforcement to become a system of control, manipulation or bribery. Let's look a little bit more at each.

The first, and main thing you need to remember is that Positive Reinforcement should be geared toward Behaviors, not children per se. It is not a substitute for responsible and caring stewardship and Leadership of children. Positive Reinforcement is a tool, as I have stated before, and you can't dump a pile of tools and raw materials on an empty lot and come back and expect a house to have assembled itself. You need skilled and dedicated workers, who use the tools to help construct a house. In a group setting, Positive Reinforcement can help Leaders spend their time on things like teaching, coaching, caring and, well, leading.

126

With a group of kids, a Leader can feel overwhelmed and can fall into the trap of using Positive Reinforcement as a gateway to manipulation and bribery. Begging a group of kids to go to bed and promising them a treat if they do, is not Positive Reinforcement. Giving kids treats to do things that should be the Leader's job to do is not Positive Reinforcement. Promising treats for the kids not to tell that you let them stay up late is bribery, not Positive Reinforcement. Positive Reinforcement should be planned out and well defined and used as a tool, not a crutch, and certainly, not as a replacement for Leadership.

You should set up your program to reinforce specific desired Behaviors, such as, waiting to be called on before you speak and using manners, rather than to try and get individual kids to be "good". Telling a group of kids that they will be reinforced for being good is way too general and way too subjective. One kid's idea of being good is another kid's idea of being bad. Specific Behaviors are what you should target. For instance if you were going to reinforce good manners, I would suggest having a mini class or review of what you are considering good manners and get the kids involved. Create a specific idea and set of rules defining what good manners are and what they are not. Writing this down or recording it may even be a good idea so that there is a reference to go by.

For example, if you told the kids you would be Reinforcing good manners and left it at that, then you will have as many sets of definitions as to what good manners are as you have kids. A child could purposely belch as loud as they could at the dinner table and then say "excuse me" and

127

expect to be reinforced for having the good manners to say "excuse me". Maybe that is good manners where he comes from. You could even give this set of agreed to manners another name, such as, camp manners or something unique so there is no other set of manners that it can be compared to.

For whichever Behaviors you target, you are going to have kids that are lower achievers. Some will be lower achievers because they have made a choice and are being defiant or are trying to gain peer attention by being too cool to participate. Maybe they have anxiety about their ability and are not trying for fear of failure. Another thing you must watch for are kids that want to do what is asked, but lack the ability to do so. Look for all these kids and if they need help, spend time with them and build them up. If they have the ability but choose not to, for whatever reason, let them know they are losing out on the Reinforcer, not hurting you or anyone else. Don't make it about you and them, they should be competing with themselves to earn the Reinforcers for themselves.

Having more than one child involved in your Positive Reinforcement program drastically alters the dynamics in many different ways. First of all, the Behaviors you can reinforce as well as the pool of via Reinforcers decrease as group size increases. Furthermore, this is true when additional demographics are added to the mix. Once you add a boy to a mix that was previously all girls then the previous Reinforcer or Reinforcers may not be sufficient. Same goes with adding kids of different ages, socioeconomic backgrounds, skill levels, or any other variables that make the performance of target Behaviors easier or more difficult for some children and the existing Reinforcers not desirable or

128

appropriate. Older kids may not be motivated by stuffed animals, girls may not be motivated by wrestling action figures, children in remedial classes may not be able to achieve academic Behavioral goals, and these are just some of the many possible challenges to consider once you add that second child.

Having common goals can be a good thing if done right. The same goes with competition. You want the group supporting its individuals and more able to help the less able. If you aren't cognizant of this up front when you are setting it up, you may have kids with less ability having no chance against kids with more ability and, in the end, provide little challenge for the higher achiever and a blow to self-esteem for the lower achiever. The best competition is the one where the kids compete against themselves as individuals to benefit the group. For instance, the kids take a baseline test at the beginning of the program and earn points for their group as they better their score against their own initial score.

You can design your program where it is a bunch of individuals working toward their own Reinforcers without any impact to the group. You can also set it up so that the individual's achievement of the desired Behaviors contributes toward the group's attainment of Reinforcers. Finally, you can create a mix or hybrid of the two. Its best to examine what Behaviors you want to target and then look at the mix of kids you will be working with and try the setup you estimate will be most effective. Of course, you then implement, track, measure, evaluate and finally, tweak.

Individual Behavior independent group Reinforcement is a

bunch of individuals working on their own Behavior for themselves to earn Reinforcers. With this, you have the advantage of not having to worry about an individual or subgroup being used as a scapegoat for the failure of the larger group from achieving the goal. You also have the downside of not being able to utilize the momentum, motivation and synergy that can be gained from a shared goal and the support and camaraderie between individuals whose outcome is shared. An example of a group of individuals would be a teacher Reinforcing the completion of a project early by giving an extra recess time to anyone who turned it in by a certain date while the other kids who didn't, had to stay in the classroom and work on their project. Each child determines whether or not they earn the Reinforcer, and whether they do or not is not affected by the actions of their classmates, nor do their actions affect their classmates' opportunity to earn the Reinforcer.

You can set up a program, which we will call Subgroup Behavior Dependent Group Reinforcement where a subgroup of the larger group or even just one kid's Behavior determines if the larger group earns a Reinforcer. This can be a powerful additional motivator for the subgroup or kid tasked with performing the desired Behavior as the whole classroom can exert support and positive peer pressure. The downside of this is if the subgroup, or child, fails to perform the desired Behavior then they have not only not changed their own Behavior, but have let down a large group of their peers who may now be resentful, which can be a blow to the self-esteem of the kids in the subgroup and could lead to them blaming one other. An example may be selecting five kids from a summer camp group to learn how to tie an intricate knot and if they do it, then the whole group gets ice cream at the end of the week. Personally, another example would be a high school sports team who can win glory or shame for their entire school. I feel the downside to this sort of program would almost always be too great a risk for me to use this method, but I'm sure there are situations out there in which this setup would be desirable.

Individual behavior dependent group Reinforcement is where the collective sum of Behavior of the whole group determines whether or not the group as a whole earns the Reinforcer. This has the advantage or the whole group pulling together toward a shared cause. The downside is that if the group falls short, it could begin the blame game and the camaraderie that was built as the group was working together can be torn down and replaced with accusations and animosity. An example of this may be a class of kids trying to reach a target number of reading points by a certain date where books anyone in the classroom reads count towards the goal and a group Reinforcer of a party is at stake. Overachievers can excel and have their effort lifting the class instead of having be competitive as it may otherwise be.

You also have Group behavior dependent group reinforcement. This is where the program rules and desired Behaviors are the same for the whole group and the entire group earns Reinforcers based on the combined Behavior of the whole group. Individual performance is lumped together and tracked collectively and that combined metric is used to determine if the group has earned a Reinforcer. The difference

---

CHAPTER 1 QUIZ ANSWER

4) Kevin was the coach of his son's little league team. The kids were not hitting the ball very well so he decided to try something. Before each child got up to bat, Kevin pulled them aside and told them something positive like "I know you can do this" or "I believe in you". He did this for every batter every time they got up to bat. Sure enough, the kids batting average when up as a team over the course of the next week.

Is this an example of positive reinforcement?

The answer was no.

Many of you said yes because the encouraging message sounded positive and led to better hitting. This was however not Positive Reinforcement because the pep talk occurred before the behavior and was not contingent on the behavior occurring. While confidence building talk is helpful and in this instance successful, it is not what we are specifically look for.

---

between this and Individual behavior dependent group Reinforcement is that as the names imply, one tacks the performance of the group as a whole without distinguishing individual performance, while the other is the sum of all the individual totals which are tracked and known.

Many times a Positive Reinforcement program set up for a group of kids has the goal of seeing an increase of a few target Behaviors, which also usually results in the decrease of some other related Behaviors. This is pretty straight forward, but you should be sure to think through what you anticipate it looking like with your specific set of kids, so it doesn't create situations you don't want. Even with a simple program, it is important to write out in advance, including what your goals and objectives are so you can make sure you have set up a system which will allow your kids to achieve success.

Here are some questions to ask at the beginning. This is not meant as an all-inclusive list, but rather, as an exercise to help spark the questions that will be meaningful for your particular group, and are in addition to the steps outlined in chapter 11:

Siblings

We could be dealing with a group as small as two when dealing with siblings, but it is still a group, and it is important to get the family involved and behind the program. The easiest way to do this with a sibling is to get them participating too. You can find a Behavior for them and reinforce them at a rate relative to their sibling's Reinforcement in difficulty, adjusting for age, and how difficult the Behavior is for that given child. I would recommend involving them, but if you can't do that then you should make sure they are supportive of the program and not jealous of it.

The same rules apply for programs for siblings as they do for groups as discussed earlier in the chapter. Competition can work depending on the dynamic of the siblings you are working with or could be highly counterproductive. In either case, as a Caregiver you should be especially cognizant of its existence or potential existence. Highly competitive kids who take competition too seriously could have totally different programs so that they seem like apples it oranges when compared, but both can be happy with the fact that they each have an opportunity to earn Reinforcers. On the other hand, sometimes competition is healthy and can push siblings to succeed and may be a channel for some existing competitive tension that already existed to be released.

Working toward common or group objectives to earn Reinforcers can build the relationship of the siblings through cooperation. It can also be an issue if one sibling can dominate the other in some shape or form. For instance, an older brother could get very aggravated with a younger sibling who does not do what they need to do to earn a Reinforcer. The flip side when the opposite happens, if the dominated sibling will not have the ability to exert their influence on the dominating sibling to get them to do what they need to do when they don't feel like it and so would be at their mercy. In any case the Caregiver should monitor this closely and make sure it doesn't become a problem for either child.

At the end of the day, whether you are talking about two kids or fifty, the introduction of a second child creates a group dynamic that must be accounted for. This can make the job or the Caregiver easier, harder, or both. Human beings are social creatures and how we act or behave when we are alone, or in the case of children, away from other kids, is often different that how we act or behave when peers are around. This is not necessarily a bad thing but simply a set of variables that must be accounted for as Caregivers implementing Positive Reinforcement.

Questions for Group Positive Reinforcement

--How many behaviors do we want to reinforce?

--How many behaviors could the group leadership track at any one time?

--Is this a behavior that needs to be externally reinforced?

--What would a successful execution of the desired behavior look like and/or what specifically must happen and/or not happen for it to qualify for a reinforcer?

--Will all the leaders, who will distribute reinforcers, be able to identify a success consistently and also with the same approximation with the other leaders?

--Can the group leadership track behavior and if so, how will track behavior?

--Will it be too easy for some kids?

--Will it be too hard for some kids?

--What are the pros and cons for this group of competition and cooperation?

CHAPTER 13:

Applications by Age Group

How you handle Positive Reinforcement with a toddler, is obviously different from how you handle it with a teenager. There are no hard and fast rules, as each child is different in ways such as maturity and social skills, and so many factors that can affect how you should approach it. There are some generalities that can be applied to age groups however, that can be used as a baseline, or starting point, with a child and can be tweaked according to their, and your, needs.

A few universals regardless of age:

- ⚔ Always start with the goal of the child developing the Behavior and having the Reinforcement come from within the child. If they are doing something, and they are doing it because they are interested in it or because it brings them joy, then there is nothing to modify and the adage, if it ain't broke, don't fix it, applies. This is where you want to get your kids to and if they are there already, then work on providing them opportunities or scenarios to do it rather than worry about Reinforcing it.

⅄ If they are not doing the desired Behavior then you want to use Positive Reinforcement to get them to start, and help them transition to an internal Reinforcement so that the external Reinforcement is eventually no longer needed.

⅄ Don't use Reinforcement for goals or objectives other than encouraging desired Behaviors.
  ◦ For instance don't give your child a sticker for going to get you a coke when they are supposed to be earned for cleaning up after they eat.
  ◦ Don't try and bribe your kids with Reinforcers like giving them some points in their Token Economy if they agree not to tell Mom you didn't remember to fix the lawnmower.
  ◦ Don't use Reinforcers in lieu of parenting because it is convenient. For instance, don't give them a Reinforcer for promising not to lie anymore. You can't reinforce Behavior that has not happened yet.

⅄ No matter what the age, if the Reinforcers are not sufficiently motivating then the Reinforcement will not be as effective or may not work at all.

⅄ Clearly defined Behaviors, and what constitutes a success and what does not, is crucial so that the child never feels cheated or tricked.

⅄ Consistency and dedication on the part of the Caregiver is critical. Consistency means doing what you are supposed to do based on how the program was explained to the child, and it is critical. Now granted, this does not mean that they necessarily get a Reinforcer every time, you may be on a different Schedule of Reinforcement. The Schedule should have been explained as part of the explanation of the program and it is that explanation that you need to be consistent on. You must also be dedicated to follow through, day in and day out, or the program will deteriorate and fall apart.

⅄ If Positive Reinforcement is the only parenting tool in your toolbox and everything is one hundred percent fine and your child is a perfect angel then I say congratulations, I hope it lasts for you. If you are like the rest of us, parenting is a constantly changing job that requires a lot of research, education and on the job training. Don't get me wrong, Positive Reinforcement can be extremely useful, but you should look to be constantly expanding your repertoire of skills and tools.

2-3 Toddlers

A toddler isn't going to understand a complex program or Token Economy, and may not have the skills to delay gratification long enough to work towards larger Reinforcers. The good news is you can usually just concentrate on explaining the desired Behavior  without worrying about the program. More good news is children of this age may very well be happy with stickers or praise as a Reinforcer. For both of my boys, when they were very young, I would buy sheets of stickers of Pokemon© or dinosaurs and when they earned one of these it was a huge deal for them.

Again, just to reiterate, these are just some ideas thrown down as a baseline. You know your child or children and will have to use your best judgment coupled with experimentation to find out what works and what does not.

4-5 Preschool Years

Children in the preschool years may be motivated by the same things as some toddlers and be happy with praise and simple Reinforcers such as  stickers. Children at this age are sometimes able it grasp simple Token Economies such as a chart with spaces for stickers or check marks that get filled as they do the desired Behavior with the Primary Reinforcer being earned when the chart is full.

Something you are going to want to be aware of if they go to daycare or pre-school is if a Positive Reinforcement program is being used there. It is often easier for the Caregiver, as well as for the child, if the home system is the same or similar to the one used in school or wherever. The Behaviors can be different of course as long as they are not contradicting, but the system should be the same or similar.

6-8 Primary School Years

Once children start more formalized schooling there is a very

good chance that they will be part of a Positive Reinforcement program there. Again, piggybacking off that program can make life easier for everyone involved. Children at these ages are often strongly influenced by the approval of Caregivers, so praise and recognition can go a long way.

Children at these ages are pretty sophisticated, so a more elaborate Token Economy can be used and multiple Behaviors can be targeted at the same time as well. In my personal experience, children of this age develop a keen sense of justice and injustice. Where you may have gotten away with forgetting a day or something like that when they were younger, they will probably call you out on it now. Consistency and dedication as a Caregiver are again key.

9-12 Tween Years

These are the years where generally more complex peer relationships are formed, and the peer's approval can rival or exceed the Caregiver's approval in the eyes of the child. Your public praise may be welcome and reassuring for some kids or awkward and  embarrassing for others. Don't design your program to try and change or test the nature of your relationship with your child. Positive Reinforcement should free up some of your time that you would have spent dealing with a Behavior so that you can use it for things like building your relationship with your child.

Kids at these ages are pretty sophisticated and know what they want and what motivates them. Explain the program more to children of this age and explain the goal of wanting these Behaviors to become habits and that they won't be reinforced forever. Coach and teach them often about how they may feel as sense of satisfaction from performing the target Behavior or one like it. Help them find their inner satisfaction and Reinforcement from doing the Behavior.

13-15 Early Teens

Luckily, teenagers are easy, and a joy to deal with at all times. Ha. OK they can be challenging. They are super smart but have zero experience and know you inside and out, flaws and all. Nature has wired them to rebel and break away, so they will venture into the world. Nature has also wired us Caregivers to try and keep them protected and away from the  world as long as possible. You hope you don't kill each other and prepare them the best you can for the day they will go out into the world.

Positive Reinforcement should only be one tool you utilize at this age. It can still be very effective but don't think a sticker

144

chart is going to win them over. Here, is where I need to remind you that adults participate willingly and happily every day in Token Economies. Companies spend millions and millions of dollars on point programs and frequent shopper programs and Reward programs. I say this in case you are thinking that your teen is just too big for this Positive Reinforcement stuff. Too big for what you did when they were younger, but not too big for Positive Reinforcement.

You certainly don't want to do anything that will be embarrassing to them. For instance, for some kids, a big wall chart that their friends could see when they come over would be humiliating, while for other kids, it may be further Reinforcing. Same thing with giving teens tickets or point cards out in public or when friends are around. You will have to discover what works best for your child here. Maybe throughout the day you do subtle acknowledgments of target Behaviors exhibited or opportunities missed or for some Behaviors and/or kids maybe this is not necessary. You could do a nightly or weekly evaluation that is like a scorecard reviewing how they are doing and equating to points or whatever. You can even have them do self-evaluations that let them talk about their view of their performance and how they can improve. Again, experiment and go with what works.

16-18 High School Years

This is the age group that will be potentially rebelling the hardest, so you need to make sure you get their buy-in and have a sufficient Reinforcer. Not to beat a dead horse, but you know your child best and have the best idea of where to start and what might work, knowing even if you are wrong, you can always change it up until you find that magic mix. I would recommend that you start looking to programs aimed at adults as models for what may work for your teen.

Programs aimed at adults are straight forward for the most part and don't hide what it is they want you do. They also stress the "Reward" and so they make sure their Reinforcers are motivating and then promote them. The thing that many adult targeted programs do a horrible job at doing is creating actual Behavior change. That is not to say they don't create Behavior change at all but in my experience, they don't do a very good job of pointing out the benefits of the new Behavior and instead rely on the program itself to be the impetus of the Behavior rather than the adults doing it because it is right for them, or some way advantageous, even without the "Reward".

Many times they count on the fact that people don't want to lose what they have invested into the program. For instance, they stay with their "loyalty" program because they are loyal to the points they have in their bank and become a lot less "loyal" right after they use them to redeem for a "Reward". This is not how you want to run your program for your teen. Use what works in these glitzy programs like the appropriate Rewards, clearly spelled out Behavior expectations, and marketing of the Reinforcer, making sure the audience not only wants it, but wants it badly.

You want to make sure the new Behaviors become self-rewarding so they will continue after your program ends, whether it is something that becomes self-evident as the right thing to do, beneficial in some way to them, someone or something they care about or simply because a new habit is formed. No matter which, it may be a good suggestion to do as the old saying suggests and lead your horse to water but don't make them drink. In other words, you need them to make the connection, whatever it may be, that it is in their best interest to continue the desired Behavior, even after it is no longer being reinforced. If this linkage is not established then all you have done is created a "loyalty" program that keeps your teen loyal to it as long as you are giving them Tokens, and only as long as they live with you. Our job is to prepare them for the world, not just living under our roof.

Conclusion

All in all, you must remember these are suggestions and the ages are rough guidelines. I'm not trying to cop out here, but each child will respond differently to different strategies, and even though a child has a given chronological age, their maturity age may be older or younger and thus effect what will be effective with them. Use your intimate knowledge of your child to help guide your initial program or strategy, but after that, whenever you tweak you program rely more and more on the data of what works, and less and less on your thoughts based on your knowledge of your child. You need to rely on your knowledge of them when you're beginning your program, but it is essential that you let that weigh less and less as you collect data through tracking results. You will discover that you can actually learn things about your child and your relationship that you would not have been able to learn otherwise

CHAPTER 14:

Applications by Setting

As we have discussed, Positive Reinforcement works in a variety of settings, from you and your child in your own home, to an adult charged with watching or leading a group of kids, who are unknown to them. Positive Reinforcement has various advantages, roles and challenges, depending of the specific setting, application and specific group of kids. Sometimes Positive Reinforcement is one of many care-giving tools available and just happens to be the best fit for the situation and other times Positive Reinforcement is the only tool available to the Caregiver and must be tweaked to work in the given situation. On top of the basics of how to implement a program, and the considerations of a group settings and children of different ages, sometimes the setting itself must be considered. This may be advantageous or present other challenges that must be dealt with.

Babysitting

If you are using an existing Positive Reinforcement program, then you should educate your babysitters if you want them to track the target Behaviors. They could report to you when

Be Good for the Babbysitter!

you come back to relieve them. I would not recommend this unless you use the same babysitter and use them regularly. A potential problem is that they don't know the program like you do and may not grade on the same curve, so to speak, and their idea of a success may not be yours.

If your kids are like mine, then you are happy if the babysitter is able to survive the night, no one is hurt, and the house is not burned down. Here are a couple ideas that you could use with a babysitter.

New or not often used sitter:

If they are new or you don't use them often, then you could make a list of problem Behaviors that occur when the babysitter is there, and list their opposites on a chart. So, if jumping on the sofa is a problem the chart could have a spot that says kept feet off the couch the whole night. There could also be a few "spot" awards that the babysitter could use to ad-lib. For instance, they could offer a sticker on the chart for picking up all the scattered puzzle pieces and putting the box back where it belonged.

A filled out chart could earn a Reinforcer or better yet, different amounts of Token stickers earn different tier Reinforcers so the more they earn, the better the Reinforcer. You could also have an ongoing babysitter chart broken up into grids of ten squares, where they earn a Reinforcer every time a grid section is filled with stickers. You could come up with custom Reinforcers just for babysitting night which will lend them an air of specialness. You could have it earn Tokens in your regular system, as well. Experiment and see what works best.

Organized Groups

There are a lot of themed group activities for kids. Some examples would be Scouting, Church groups, chorus or band groups, clubs, or anything that gathers a group of children for some non-sporting purpose. These generally can be categorized into two separate types, those organized around a central activity or theme, such as a chess club, and those organized around a system or set of beliefs or rules such as Scouts.

A good rule of thumb for both types is to not set your Positive Reinforcement program up around the activity or the central system, beliefs or rules. You don't want to reinforce playing chess for the chess club because this is the reason for the club and should already be intrinsically Reinforcing. Now, if you wanted to reinforce children being quiet when people are in a match, that is a different story. You don't want to reinforce earning a rank in scouting, because the rank is already a Reinforcer. If you wanted to reinforce lining up in an orderly fashion and you couldn't find something governing or reinforcing that within the group's existing system, then that may be a candidate.

While you don't want to reinforce Behavior that is part of the reason for the group, there is nothing wrong with using a Reinforcer that fits the activity or the culture of the system. You want to ensure that there is no rule against it or contradiction, and that it doesn't detract or distract away from anything the system is doing.

I was a den Leader in scouting for my son's first grade Scouting group. I found a great idea online of a Reinforcement system using beads. I modified it to what I wanted and had them decorate a block of wood with a hole drilled through it so it could fit on a long bolt and be secured to a display stand made of wood. The boys hung their blocks, which they decorated themselves, with their name on it and two leather cords hanging off the bottom. When they correctly performed certain target Behaviors, they earned a special bead from the big bag of elaborate beads I bought at the craft store. The number and types of beads were a status symbol and the boys competed to earn them and were thrilled when they got them. Several Parents were amazed and commented on how effective this was as the year went on.

Sports Teams

Sports teams are basically also groups based around a theme, but there are enough of them, and there are enough differences, even if they are subtle, that it is worth mentioning them in a separate section. For one thing, sports are already competitive, so you may want to make your Reinforcement program more individual oriented, so that the kids are not competing with one another. That is not always easy, and while you want to base the program around Behaviors, if you can stay true to that and have some of the kids who aren't the top athletes come out ahead, then that may be beneficial.

Individual behavior dependent group Reinforcement programs can be effective team builders if set up properly. One idea that is a little complicated but could be very effective  for a little league team is to establish a set of baseline scores, or times or whatever for each kid. There could be timed running, a quiz about situations, how well they hit ten pitches or some basic exercises, etc. The kids could compete against their own baseline scores and some measure of their improvement could be used to earn "runs" for the team, and when the team hit certain "run" level there would be a team Reinforcer like an ice cream party, or no laps after practice, or something that is Reinforcing.

Each child is competing against themselves, and the whole team is motivated to support the improvement of each player against a mark that is fair and attainable for them. Ideally in this system each child would further be reinforced that it is themselves who must strive to be better than and when they do that, the whole team wins. While individual kids could still fail to progress, it would not be because another child was better than them, but because they didn't work to improve themselves, and that should hold a lesson as well.

Educational

Many Educators, from pre-school to high school, have embraced Positive Reinforcement and Token Economies for several decades. You may have experienced this first hand while in school and if not, there is a good chance your children are being positively reinforced as they go to school now. How to run a Positive Reinforcement program as an educator deserves its own book, so I will not jump into that here. I will discuss it from the other side of the equation, as the Caregiver of a child in school.

For Caregivers of children in school, there are a couple different scenarios that may be encountering. You may have some Behaviors you want to target at school and there is a Positive Reinforcement program at school already. You may have some Behaviors you want to target at school and there is not a Positive Reinforcement program at school already. You may not have any Behaviors you want to target at school, but there is a Positive Reinforcement program at school. Of course, the final is you don't have any school Behaviors to work on and there is no program at school but it doesn't make any sense for us to cover that one.

If you want to target some school Behaviors it is important to find out if they have a Positive Reinforcement program in your child's class and if so, what Behaviors are they addressing? You should have in mind what Behavior or Behaviors you would like to reinforce and set up a meeting with the teacher. You will want to center the meeting on the Behaviors you want to target and then address the Positive Reinforcement as a proposed solution when appropriate in the conversation. Teachers have varying opinions about Positive Reinforcement, just as any other people do, and so it's good to get a feeling for where they sit on the subject.

Behaviors that happen strictly at home, such as the completion of homework, should be handled at home.

Behaviors that occur strictly at school, such as talking in class, should be discussed with the teacher in order to work out a plan of action. If they have a program, this Behavior may already be in the process of being addressed. The teacher may be willing to try Positive Reinforcement with your child but as they have a whole classroom of kids to consider, it would be unreasonable to expect them to do it just for your child outside a program covering the whole class.

Many Behaviors that become problematic are the ones that overlap school and home, precisely because they span two or more of the child's Caregivers spheres of control and or responsibility. I found that these usually center on a breakdown of the communication system in one form or another. Some examples may be not getting their homework agenda filled out or brought home or signed and returned. All of these are communication issues as the child is the courier of information, and if they don't do their job all else breaks down. Many schools have homework information online so things like this are not as much of a problem, but in my experience, paperwork still must go back and forth from home and school.

You must be willing to work with the school and the teachers, and you may have to meet them half way. If there is a Behavior being reinforced at school and it a Behavior that you currently are, or plan to, reinforce at home, it is much more realistic to build off of, and support, the school program than to expect the opposite when they have a whole group of kids they must work with. It is also confusing to the children to treat the Reinforcement of a Behavior differently, including the Reinforcer or the definition of what constitutes a success.

155

So work with your teachers and be willing to support their program with your program to ensure the best results. If your child's school or teacher makes special accommodations, whether informal or formal, such as the Individualized Education Plan ("IEP") used in American schools, then you should actively speak about Positive Reinforcement at your meetings with educators as well as work with the individual teachers to implement it with your child. You don't need a formal plan (IEP or other) however, to get a teacher to work with you. Teachers are people too, and usually people who have the best hopes and wishes for your child and work very hard toward that end, so support them, and work with them and in return, they will likely work with you.

Conclusion

You must remember your goal when using Positive Reinforcement, and that is to create a change in Behavior. Your goal is not to implement a Reinforcement program run in a specific way. Different settings effect how you run your program, whether we are talking about an existing program for a single child entering a different setting or whether you are creating a program for a group of kids in a new setting. You will be much more successful if you conform your program to the setting instead of vice versa and utilize what the setting has to offer. The setting may offer, built in, Positive Reinforcement or established Reinforcers or something else that may help you. Be sure not to contradict the rules or customs of the setting and to be complimentary to them in what you do.

CHAPTER 15:

What Works and Measuring Effectiveness

Positive Reinforcement for Kids: The adding of a result or consequence that the child finds pleasant, dependent on the occurrence of a certain Behavior or Response by the child, which results in an increase in the likelihood of that Behavior or Response in the child, because of the added result or consequence.

That is our working definition from chapter one. An important phrase in that sentence that is often overlooked is, "which results in an increase in the likelihood of that Behavior or Response". Specifically, what is overlooked is, "results in an increase ". Most people set up the program with the intention of increasing the desired Behavior and then fall into a trap that is inherent in focusing on anything in particular, in that, they think they see more of it. If you buy a green car, then suddenly you notice green cars all over the road. Did a bunch of people buy green cars right after you did or were they always there and now you are just noticing them? If you start looking for the desired Behavior, you will start to see it, and this may incorrectly look like an increase in the Behavior.

If you want to successfully change Behavior using Positive Reinforcement you have to know if what you are doing is working or not, and if not, you will need to change it. You need to put your white lab coat on and think of this as an experiment. You have to establish a baseline and then compare the amount of the desired Behavior after you have applied Positive Reinforcement to determine if you have increased the Behavior. If it is not increasing, then you are not positively reinforcing the Behavior and should stop what you are doing. You then need to evaluate why it is not working, including looking at the Reinforcer to see if it is adequately motivating.

After you have decided what Behavior, or Behaviors you want to change or replace, then you need to take some time and measure how often the desired Behavior is exhibited. What length of time over which to record this depends on the frequency of the opportunities for the Behavior and how many varying environments that the Behavior spans.

For instance, if the desired Behavior is for them to clean their room once a week, then a couple weeks would be needed to record a trend, whereas saying thank you may present ten opportunities a day. That brings up another good point, in that, it may be more useful to record how many opportunities for the desired Behavior, as well as, the desired Behavior and record X number opportunities as opposed to a set number days. For instance you could record the next twenty opportunities to say thank you that Suzie had instead of two days of opportunities, which could produce a number much bigger or smaller than that.

160

Varying environments can make creating an accurate baseline a challenge, as well. For instance, if you are staying with relatives while on vacation, it probably would not be a good week to create a baseline. Even if you are at home, you can run into many diverse environments, such as, the grocery store, car commutes, having friends over, etc. If your life is normally chaotic and ever changing, then those are the conditions that will produce a good baseline, but it may take a couple weeks. If you find you are in the midst of an unusual week, then it is probably best to just skip it and wait for a more normal week.

Besides giving you the ability to determine if the Behavior is increasing, decreasing or remaining the same, a baseline will also help you set targets or goals. Depending on the Behavior, the circumstances and the child, you may want to reinforce a certain number of Behaviors for the day. Maybe the child exhibits the Behavior half the time when presented with the opportunity and you want closer to 100%. You could reinforce each time they do it over the minimum threshold you set which could be the baseline or better yet, just below the baseline to encourage them and help them build momentum.

Once you have your baseline, you know how often to expect that desired Behavior when you do nothing, or at least when you do what you normally do. Now you can implement the Positive Reinforcement and measure again to see if it increases. Don't stop measuring if it does increase, continue to gather data. It is important to know when the Behavior has plateaued and when it drops off, which may signal Satiation or, if you have removed the Reinforcer, Extinction. Tracking

161

success is good feedback for your child, as well.

	A	B	C	D	E
1	Date	Number of Times Left Room	Number of Times Turned Light Off	Percentage	
2	01/01/13	15	5	33.33%	
3	01/02/13	17	7	41.18%	
4	01/03/13	12	4	33.33%	
5	01/04/13	17	7	41.18%	
6	01/05/13	25	11	44.00%	
7	01/06/13	11	5	45.45%	
8	01/07/13	17	8	47.06%	
9	01/08/13	11	6	54.55%	
10	01/09/13	12	6	50.00%	
11	01/10/13	22	12	54.55%	
12	01/11/13	18	11	61.11%	
13	01/12/13	19	10	52.63%	
14	01/13/13	7	4	57.14%	
15	01/14/13	20	14	70.00%	
16					

To track all this data you can use any number of things. You can jot it down on paper or put it in an elaborate spreadsheet. How you track it is not nearly as important as, are you tracking, and tracking accurately. With a spreadsheet, you can take the data and make some fancy pie charts and graphs. That is great, but you need to collect the data before you can display the data. One easy method is to carry a small spiral notebook, the very small ones that fit into a pocket, and keep it with you to record successes. One of my favorites is the cell phone. I always have mine, so I find it easy to use the note function, send a text to my email, or any of many different ways you can use it to track successes.

Now once you have the data, you can enter it onto the paper, spreadsheet, or whatever. One thing that works really well is a simple wall chart. We always like to have a chart with a column for each day, and there would be a sticker placed in that column for each successful Behavior. That allows you to keep track and gives your child feedback on how they are doing. If you just need to keep track of successes then this may be the method for you but if you are tracking several Behaviors and need to track opportunities so a success percentage can be figured out, then maybe a chart is not enough or won't work at all, and more elaborate means of

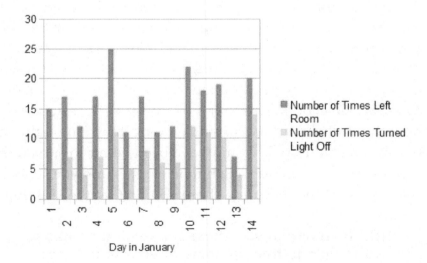

tracking and recording should be used. I always like to keep it simple, at least for the side the kids saw, and if I wanted more, I could use those means behind the scenes.

I know, I know, you are incredibly busy and all this sounds so complicated and time consuming, but it doesn't have to be. KISS can be applied here just as it can to most things in life. For those of you not familiar with the acronym, it stands for,

K eep "Keep It Simple, Stupid", which is a good philosophy for Positive Reinforcement programs. You don't want your kids scratching their heads trying to guess what they are supposed to be doing or not knowing how they earn Reinforcers, and you certainly don't need to be spending all your free time working one tracking, maintaining and reporting the results of the program.

I t

S imple

S tupid!

At one stage of my life, where I was working long hours, had a long commute and was trying to start a business on the side, you know, a typical American lifestyle, I had a stroke of genius. Now you may not agree, and may not follow my lead on this one, but it worked for me when I literally had not time to spare. One of the Behaviors I chose to transfer was a household chore I was currently doing that I thought my oldest son could do. It would have been better to spread the love to my other son as well, but he was just too young at the time. I'm sure there is some chore you do that the kids could

> **TIP: Hand one of your time consuming chores to your child to free up some of your time to run your program**

take off your hands that would allow you the time to then spend on building and Reinforcing positive Behaviors in them.

So basically, you want to track the Behavior accurately but

with minimum thought and effort. You want to track consistently, so you know if what you are doing is working. Now keep in mind, we are talking about tracking the Behavior, not reinforcing the Behavior. How and when you reinforce the Behavior will be a be a product of the things discussed earlier in the book including the Reinforcement

Positive Reinforcement, should be used to promote behaviors in the following ways:

--To encourage behaviors that that the child is unwilling to perform, afraid to perform, lacking the confidence to perform, or have yet to discover

--As a means to developing positive habits

--As a way to introduce and encourage new behavior

--As a means to replace a non desired, or less desired behavior with a desired, or more desired, behavior.

Schedule, the type of Behavior, the type of Reinforcer, the age of the child, etc. For tracking the Behavior, you want to know two things, the number of opportunities to perform the Behavior and either the number of times the desired Behavior was performed or the number of times it was not performed, which of course still gets you to the other. This is a success ratio you are essentially tracking.

Making tracking easy will ultimately depend on you and what works for you. I spoke before of using my cell phone which, I pretty much always have with me. One method may be to set up text templates that you text to yourself, your spouse or to an email account. If you have web access then, of course, you could email it etc. Many phones also have a note function that could be used too. Carrying a piece of paper or a small notebook would work for other people. No matter what you use, the bottom line is getting a real, unbiased assessment of the Positive Reinforcement you are using is essential, because if it isn't doing what it is intended to do, you are wasting your time.

CHAPTER 16:

Criticisms of Positive Reinforcement

You will see a lot of people, from psychologists to teachers to people who work in special education, rave about how wonderful Positive Reinforcement is. Not everyone is of that opinion, and there are many who argue against using Positive Reinforcement. In order to give you the full story, I will try to represent the main arguments in this chapter, and then attempt to refute them.

Positive Reinforcement is Bribery

The Criticism:

I hear this one a lot. If you think of a bribe as giving someone something of value in exchange for them doing something you desire them to do, then I would see the point, but I don't think that captures the essence of the concept of a bribe. If that is bribery, then we are all guilty of being bribed every time we cash a paycheck and we are bribing businesses when we pay them money. No, bribery is when we give someone something of value in exchange for another person doing something illegal, immoral or in some way, shape, or form, against the individual's belief system or view of what is right. Positive Reinforcement entices people to align proper values, and it Reward actions in line with those values and therefore is not bribery.

Response:

Your child may not want to clean their room but asking them to do so, or Reinforcing the Behavior, is not promoting an illegal, immoral or otherwise wrong action. Now, if you told a lie to your spouse that your child knew was a lie, and you offered them $10 to keep their mouth shut, then we are talking about a bribe. I think peer pressure is a form of bribery in that there is an implicit offer of friendship or group membership if the individual succumbs to group's pressure to do something that they know or feel to be wrong and/or harmful.

Too Much Evaluation of the Child's Actions

The Criticism:

Some worry that constantly giving children feedback on their actions is a form of moral micromanagement that prevents the child from developing their own sense of right or wrong, and good or bad. If Caregivers are always saying "good job", "way to go" and verbally praising all the actions for which they approve, then the child may come to expect and need that angel on their shoulder, so to speak, to tell them that what they did was good or right, or by inference, when nothing is said, that it is bad or wrong. The child may have their moral determination muscle retarded if not developed or atrophied if somewhat developed, when a Caregiver takes over that function. It may also take away from the child's inner growing intrinsic joy of performing the Behavior by Caregiver stealing their thunder.

This may further lead to a child being afraid, unwilling or unable to act when the Caregiver is not around to provide the constant feedback. The child could wait for that Caregiver to be around to act so that they can then receive praise. Worse yet, a child could come to justify wrong actions by saying that they didn't know it was wrong, rationalizing that no one was there to tell them that it was wrong or that another choice is right. The child then moves the responsibility of their actions or inactions onto the micromanaging Caregiver. While the intent is to positively reinforce right actions, all this evaluation of the child's actions stunts the child's moral growth and allow the child to use the lack of the Caregivers feedback as a crutch or excuse when wrong choices or Behaviors are performed.

Response:

I think the proper usage of praise is as a tool of encouragement and to help define what a success is. The child who would benefit from praise is the child who is overwhelmed by the task, or is unmotivated, or does not have confidence in their ability to perform the task. The goal of Positive Reinforcement should be to build a habit, or motivation, within the child such that the child performs the Behavior on their own at the appropriate times and is reinforced by either the doing of the Behavior and/or the successful accomplishment of the Behavior. In other words, Positive Reinforcement is successful when you no longer need Positive Reinforcement, and it needs to be implemented with that goal in mind. The child he describes seems to be on the other side of needing Positive Reinforcement.

Let's talk about some situations where that praise would be appropriate and the lack of some form of Reinforcer would not rob them of the joy of making their own choices but rather confirm, when they are not sure, that they are on the right path. My eldest son, especially when he was little, was easily overwhelmed by cleaning his room. I could ask him to clean his room and wait for him to come tell me about his success, but it would have been a long wait. He could only get past the overwhelming feeling when I would break the task into smaller sub-task and offered a Reinforcer for the successful completion of a sub-task. For instance, pick up all the red toys and put them away and then you can come share a cookie with me in the kitchen. Then, in that moment with him and the cookie, we could talk about his success when was in a receptive frame of mind.

'Positive Reinforcement is sometimes the fuel that powers the little engine "that could", toward its goal, until the little engine "does", and then can supply its own coal.'

My son couldn't see the completion of the task in his mind as I could, and instead could only see a pile of toys that would take three months to clean up. Breaking the task up into a smaller chunk made it more surmountable and the Reinforcer took him from a mental framework of paralysis, to a motivated state of doing, because he could then think about the cookie and not the pile of toys. Positive Reinforcement is sometimes the fuel that powers the little engine "that could", toward its goal, until the little engine "does", and then can supply its own coal.

The situation is not that different for children who are unmotivated or lack the confidence in their ability to complete the task. Positive Reinforcement can weigh the scale in favor of action when inaction has seemingly won the day. Positive Reinforcement can also help with reinforcing the child's thoughts away from what they would rather be doing or the negative thoughts that a lack of confidence can propagate in the mind. For a child who can clean their room and come and excitedly tell their Caregiver about their accomplishment, I agree, Positive Reinforcement would be a waste and inappropriately used. On the other hand, for a child who has not gotten to that point, Positive Reinforcement can build that interest, that confidence, that focus and lessen the overwhelm so that the Parent can help build the child up to get to that goal of a self-motivated child.

If you find your child is becoming, as the criticism claims, morally paralyzed then you should change your program to address that. You could remove your Reinforcer from "getting the right answer" and move it to the decision-making process. Of course, this would be a teaching moment as well. It really depends on the child and the situation, but you could use Shaping or Chaining to help them develop a decision making process where they have to do what needs to be done to arrive at a decision. If the child is unclear on what is a good choice vs. a bad one without your Reinforcement (i.e. praise) then some exercises involving the child making choices where there are no right and wrong answers and being reinforced to defend whatever choice thy make would help. The bottom line is again, Positive Reinforcement is a system, and if it isn't producing the results you want, you can change it to meet your needs.

Children Become Interested in Attention Rather than Activity

The Criticism:

Reinforcing children gets them interested in getting Reinforcers instead of the Behavior being reinforced. Telling a child "Good job!" when they make a sculpture out of clay make the child look for another way to be praised rather than think of creating another sculpture. Children who are praised a lot tend to stop the Behavior once the praise stops. You can only get the child to perform the desired Behavior as long as the Reinforcer is provided. Children fail to find the intrinsic value in doing the desired Behaviors just for the sake of doing them to the inner satisfaction that they can provide.

Response:

Positive Reinforcement should be a means and not an ends. It should be used to set the desired Behaviors in motion. It is important to also have an exit strategy for the Reinforcement while keeping the Behavior as part of the child's life. What's

174

missing from most examples used in the criticism, is an exit strategy.

For example, painting, for most children, would be a rewarding activity that would not need Reinforcement, but for some children, it may be something they need a push to do. The question that should be asked in the example is, why does that child need to be reinforced to paint or why isn't that child excited about painting? That is what should be addressed and Positive Reinforcement may be a tool to get the child started, so that the underlying issue can be addressed.

Let's say Cheryl has three older brothers who relentlessly teased her when she tried to draw or paint as a younger child. Later in Art class she needs encouragement, so the teacher may use Positive Reinforcement to get her to paint. Maybe she gets a piece of candy for painting a picture away from the other children where she feels surer she won't be criticized. The Reinforcement may get her to paint, where just encouragement alone would not get her started. Ideally you would praise the effort and the bravery and build her confidence until she gets to a point where a friend could see one of her paintings and have an opportunity to say something positive about it.

The methodology of building her self-esteem is not relevant here, what is relevant is that simply giving her a piece of candy for painting alone in a room would not address the underlying problem. The Behavior would stop when the Reward stopped if nothing else happened. Positive

Reinforcement is not a cure all, but as I have hit home throughout the book, it is a tool to be used in conjunction with other parenting skills.

The example of sharing can be seen the same way. If you reinforce sharing and never do anything beyond that, then some kids will never see the benefits of it. Some kids will get sharing without being reinforced. Some other kids will discover its joys and benefits only after doing it, which took the Positive Reinforcement to get them to try. The last group of kids, the ones that the example in the criticism is pointing to, will stop sharing once the Reinforcement is removed.

Why is that? Maybe they had a bad experience or experiences sharing where the children they shared with, didn't share back. Maybe some kids are inherently more selfish than others. Maybe it's a maturity issue. Whatever the answer, the bottom line is that there is an underlying issue that needs to be addressed. Positive Reinforcement can open the door to that issue, but the Caregiver must step through and help the child overcome that bad experience, or find the joy in sharing, or the maturity to let go so that they may get much more in return.

So you see, where Positive Reinforcement is touted as a cure all I will agree with criticism like this, but not because there is a flaw in Positive Reinforcement, but because the use in this situation is flawed or incomplete. If you start a car's engine, but don't put it in gear, and you never get to the store, you can't say the car is useless. The car is a perfectly good vehicle

176

to get you where you need to go but without additional steps and follow-through by the driver, it will function as it is supposed to and yet not get you any closer to your goal.

Undermines Risk Taking and Kills Creativity

The Criticism:

Reinforcing creative tasks makes kids less creative in their next task and they don't do as well as children who weren't reinforced. Reinforcement focuses the child on repeating the Behavior that was reinforced and restricts experimentation which is a key component of creativity. The child is afraid the go "outside the box" because the Reinforcer is "in the box". Taking risks in their creative process is seen as taking risks with the receipt of their Reinforcers.

Response:

This criticism can be valid if Caregivers get lazy and then would be something to lookout for. Risk taking is an important part of growth and learning, and if your Positive Reinforcement is discouraging it, then it is time to reexamine what you are doing. Creativity too, should be promoted, and if your approach is stifling it, then you need to change your approach. Again, these are misapplications of Positive Reinforcement rather than a failing of it. Children should be given a safe comfort zone to work from and then should be encouraged to go beyond it. Children can be positively reinforced to learn the basics and create the foundation of a comfort zone and it can then be used to reinforce stretching beyond those limits and growing in the process.

If and when at all possible, the components of a success should be praised or reinforced, as opposed to simply the outcome. In other words, sometimes it's more important to reinforce the trying than the successful completion. For example, a child having trouble with math may need encouragement along the way. When something is daunting or overwhelming, just getting started can seem impossible so sometimes it may be appropriate to set up Reinforcers for getting going. You may need to focus some of your Reinforcement on the completion of the problem, whether right or wrong and encourage the child, especially when wrong, as long as a good-faith effort is being put in. Just trying is often the greatest form of risk taking.

That's one scenario. There are others where the risk is not in the trying, but in the exploration and experimentation that is part of the creative process. Innovation and creativity should be encouraged not just in the arts and invention but in all we do as human beings. Just as, Positive Reinforcement, when not optimally applied, or misapplied, can discourage risk taking in lieu of the sure fire tried and true method of earning a Reinforcer, so too, it can encourage and multiply the risk taking and creativity in what our kids do.

General George S. Patton said, "Don't tell people how to do things, tell them what to do and let them surprise you with their results". There is no reason you can't Reward unconventional thinking applied to conventional situations. You could have a special Reinforcer given when your child comes up with an innovative way of doing a routine chore. Positive Reinforcement could be used to spark that creativity, but again, as a Caregiver you must help the child find the intrinsic reinforcement in this Behavior, if they don't find it

> **'Just trying is often the greatest form of risk taking.'**

themselves, so that the Positive Reinforcement can eventually be taken away and the Behavior will be a part of the child.

Removing the Reinforcer Decreases the Behavior

The Criticism:

Reinforcing a Behavior only increases its frequency of occurrence as long as the Reinforcement is present. There have been studies that show that once Reinforcement stops, the children being reinforced perform the Behavior less than a control group of children who were not reinforced to begin with. Positive Reinforcement prevents children from building their character such that they will not do the tasks they don't want to do without expecting some sort of Reward for having done it. Positive Reinforcement is not a long-term solution for Behavior change.

Response:

Positive Reinforcement should be used to encourage Behaviors the children don't necessarily like or are not  inclined to do without the Positive Reinforcement. For example, let's say you positively reinforced some children to eat escargot, and the children had all been previously offered the chance to try it for the first time and declined. You could then positively reinforce the kids to eat one properly prepared snail a day for a week. They then could go without for a week and then you could bring in some escargot during snack time and set them down explaining to the kids that the Reinforcers were no longer offered, but they could eat some if they wanted. Some kids would eat it, and that would be a success because they had added the new Behavior to their repertoire.

Granted, some kids would not eat the snails if they weren't offered the Reinforcer and some wouldn't do it even with the Reinforcer. Some Behaviors will stick with some kids and some won't. Here, is what the critics act like is a dirty little secret, Positive Reinforcement cannot change all Behavior such that any child will one day do the Behavior without an external Reinforcer. I'm OK with that. I'm even more OK with the fact that some Behaviors can be changed and stick around when the Reinforcers are removed. I'm OK with the fact that it may take a long time in some instances for that habit to build up.

Here we go, are you ready? I'm even OK with using Positive Reinforcement to get my children to do things they don't like to do but need to be done even if I will always have to reinforce the Behavior.

Doesn't Address the Cause of the Undesired Behavior

The Criticism:

Positive Reinforcement works by redirecting children away from undesired Behaviors into other Behaviors that are acceptable. It is basically a distraction so the child doesn't do the undesired Behavior, but is not a cure for that Behavior and, in fact, does not address it. As long as the undesired Behavior is left unaddressed it will be waiting there under the surface and will reappear just as soon as the distraction of the Positive Reinforcement is taken away. Positive Reinforcement is a magic trick that uses redirection to make people think something has occurred which has not.

Response:

From a technical point of view, this argument is valid and true, but only if you believe that textbook Positive Reinforcement is supposed to be a magical parenting technique that does not require any other form of parental guidance, support or teaching. If a child is talking in class and is reinforced to stop talking in class successfully, it really depends on the underlying cause of the talking as to whether it is likely to start up again when Positive Reinforcement is removed. If the kid is naturally social, then expecting him to never talk in class again is asking him to go against his nature. If the kid was seeking attention, the Positive Reinforcement may very well supply the attention being sought, and once removed, the child may, or may not, revert back, depending on whether a suitable substitute is found.

Positive Reinforcement has to be used as part of a greater plan to be success in many situations. That being said though, it is reasonable to assume that if you use Positive Reinforcement correctly and wisely that you can change the Behavior. Sometimes you have to discover the root cause in order to find an appropriate and effective new Behavior to encourage. For instance, back to the kid talking in class. If he is seeking attention, then it is important to find an alternative Behavior that is acceptable and will give him positive attention. If you do that correctly, then why would the child go back to the other Behavior as their needs are being met with the new alternative and they don't get in trouble? This is more than just the simplistic view of Positive Reinforcement that some seem to have, where you tell the child if you don't talk during class you get a piece of candy.

The critics of Positive Reinforcement act like doing anything in addition to textbook Positive Reinforcement denies that it works. If a child's Behavior is causing a problem, then doesn't it make sense to engage in a technique that makes it stop, does not strain the relationship, increases self-esteem and is relatively easy to do? It seems if you don't have to deal with the negative Behavior any more, or even as much, then you would actually have time to discover and address the underlying causes.

Sometimes the underlying root cause is simply that your child is a child and is acting like a child and in some situations that can be undesired. You don't want your child to stop acting like a child all together, just for the next ninety minutes. The criticism above gives us the option of addressing the underlying Behavior or perhaps reconsidering if the request is reasonable. OK, so I need to get through a boring appointment with two kids tagging along and the critics would tell me my only options are to address the underlying cause of a child being bored when asked to be quiet and do nothing for what to them is an eternity or I should admit that it is unreasonable to think that they are capable it behaving

Positive Reinforcement is flexible

and just let them run amok. Really? The underlying problem is that the kids are kids, and that is something you wouldn't want to change even if you could.

Positive Reinforcement is flexible and easy to implement on short notice when necessary. It allows the Caregiver to quickly address the Behavior and frees up resource to discover or address underlying issues. It allows Caregivers to achieve results that are measurable and quantifiable, while still being easy enough to pull off in our crazy busy lives as Parents in the modern world. Whether a Behavior is one which needs to be changed, one that needs to just be controlled, or whether you just need to get through a situation and don't care about addressing Behavior per se, Positive Reinforcement works.

Positive Reinforcement is Conditional Approval

The Criticism:

Positive Reinforcement sends the message to children that your attention, love and support are conditional on their performing certain Behaviors, doing certain things, saying certain things etc. As Caregivers, we should send the message that our attention, love and support are unconditional, and that we are there for them no matter what. Instead of Reinforcing Behavior, we should simply point out the consequences, effect or ramifications of the Behavior so the child can then feel for themselves that it was a worthy Behavior. Instead of always evaluating we can simply reflect back what the child did or said without value judgments or perhaps say nothing at all and let the child discover the positive impact of having done the Behavior. We should talk less and ask more questions to draw out the child so that they voluntarily discuss their accomplishments.

Response:

I've said this before too, but if you find that your children are seeing your Positive Reinforcement as conditional love, then you are doing it horribly wrong. I absolutely agree that children need unconditional love and support but, I also absolutely reject the notion that Positive Reinforcement and unconditional love and support are mutually exclusive. If you are only expressing love and support by praising "successful" accomplishments, then perhaps I could see the point in this criticism and I would recommend, not that that Parent stop praising their child, but that they seek some help in showing love, affection and support.

The critic above suggests instead of praising an accomplishment that there are alternatives such as saying nothing. To me, that is ignoring a Behavior, and that is a way to discourage it. Now, if a child scoops a spoonful of peas into their mouth that is usually not an accomplishment worthy of praise, but if your child has been struggling in math and you positively reinforced a study program then the child gets an A on a big test, are they saying we should just not say anything?

The next suggestion is to simply reflect back what you saw. I think this can work because by describing the success you are basically positively reinforcing it by giving the child attention, proving that you were paying attention and that you care about what they are doing. The next part of their suggestion is to simply point out the consequences, effects and/or ramifications of their action. I'm guessing that too will make the child feel good about having done the Behavior, as again, you would have showed you care, are paying attention, and you are adding the other positive results of the Behavior. After all that, I would venture to guess that the child would feel good about doing it. Am I missing something here or are they suggesting Positive Reinforcement is a good substitute for Positive Reinforcement?

The third alternative is to talk less and ask more. Again,

asking the child what part of their drawing you like best is just giving the child a different Reinforcer but, at the end of the day, it is Positive Reinforcement. Perhaps, if this criticism was reworked as a list of suggestions for improving Positive Reinforcement then it could be quoted in another section of the book. I would agree that simply saying good job when you child has created something, is lazy and a weak Reinforcer. Asking questions shows, again, that you are paying attention and care about them and what they are doing. Questions also tell them that you care what they think, and these are all things that will positively reinforce that child.

There are no doubt are other criticisms of Positive Reinforcement and maybe some better arguments or examples for the criticisms brought up. I went with the criticisms I have come across the most, and while some valid points are raised, at least in my mind, the debate was far from won by the critics. Positive Reinforcement should be used correctly and with purpose. It should also not be seen as an end all, be all parenting strategy, but it can be an extremely effective one that works in most situations While it is not perfect, it is useful and flexible and most importantly, effective.

CHAPTER 17:

Graduation

The last chapter dealt with criticisms of Positive Reinforcement, and it was the longest chapter in the book. I'd like to also think that the criticisms were honestly approached and refuted. Even though we are able to counter the critic's arguments you will still find people who will not try Positive Reinforcement and say it is because it doesn't work. I find that to be ridiculous as it doesn't take thousands of dollars or years of time to give it a try. In fact, it can be done with no money and just a few hours of time. Given the potential upside I can't think of a reason not to give it a shot, and if you can't get it to work with your child, then just stop using it.

Some critics may examine what I'm saying and be quick to point out that I am not a purist. I don't say that any and every Behavior can be changed with Positive Reinforcement, and I also say that many Behaviors take more than just Reinforcers if you want permanent change. Guilty as charged. Just using Positive Reinforcement in the strictest sense will work many times, but I believe, and have seen it work first hand, that if you do more, you often get better and longer lasting results. I don't think it is a philosophical departure from the basic theory to suggest that we, as parents, add thought and analysis to the Positive Reinforcement, to make it more effective. I am a parent and I'm interested in results and what is best for my children and what will help me raise them the best way I can.

To deny there are limitations in any system is folly, but to throw it out entirely because of them is foolish. You may not be able to build an entire house with just a hammer, but it's a hell of a lot easier to build one if you do have a hammer. Positive Reinforcement is not going to be the sole cure for every problem, but it is nice to have in your repertoire when you have a problem that it will work on. It may not work on every child at every age, but I think you have to prove that on the child that matters to you.

You have to ask yourself if you are looking for a religion, or a parenting technique. There are plenty of parenting religions, and even more parenting prophets proclaiming you do it this way and you raise perfect children and you never have to do anything else. You may even find a prophet of Positive Reinforcement, but I would urge caution. Anything that is one size fits all, usually fits few or none. Some kids, in some circumstances, at certain ages, will respond perfectly to Positive Reinforcement and may not need anything else. Enjoy it while it lasts because they will need more, and to be honest, you need more too so that you can grow as Parents, and they as children. The world is variety and so should be our parenting techniques.

When trying to deal with a problem Behavior or trying to

teach a new Behavior, it is important to figure out what your goals are, what constitutes a success, what are the obstacles and how much or how little your child wants to change or learn the Behavior? Sometimes just getting them to try something is enough. Exposure to new and different things is a key to a well-rounded child.

Sometimes just getting them to do something is the goal. For other things, you don't care or have time for a major life lesson. Some things just need to be done, or you just need to get through them. In the real-world, most parents want to have a positive impact on their children as much as the Parents in the academic world that talk about the Parents we should be. Real world Parents need to pick their battles, choose their moments, decide on which moments are teaching moments, and the rest of the time they need a method, or technique, to get done what needs to get done. Having a system in place that you are ready to use and that is flexible can be a safety net, so that in a stressful moment we have a go-to plan other than yelling, using guilt, threat of Punishment, intimidation, giving them control to make bad choices, or any other bad parenting trap that we can fall into if not prepared.

The question is, are you looking for Behavior modification or Behavior change? You can modify a Behavior for a while, or you can change it permanently. Behavior change takes more thought, more effort and usually, but not always, more time. The wonderful thing about Positive Reinforcement is that you can use it to accomplish either. Even complex Behaviors can be learned or changed using methods like Chaining and Shaping. Positive Reinforcement is flexible enough to work on the smallest Behaviors or the most complex, and on very young children just as well as older children, or even adults.

Is it effective? That is the question, and there is a ton of evidence to say yes, it is. Is it effective for your child? That is really the question and while there may not be any evidence that proves it is, there is this wonderful laboratory called your life, and for very little investment of your time and possibly but not necessarily some money, you can empirically prove the answer one way or the other.

The next question then is, can it be harmful? Looking at the worst of the criticisms and assuming them to be correct, let's see how badly you could mess up your child. The Behavior you are trying to change or get them to learn may or may not be changed, or learned, which puts you right back to where you started anyway. Let's say it decreases intrinsic motivation and/or creativity. Don't try it on creative activities and you shouldn't be using it on Behaviors the child is already intrinsically motivated to perform. So really you have nothing to lose in giving it a try.

One thing I did was, examine my sons' lives and discovered that what I saw as their privileges, they saw as their entitlements. I should take a step back and point out that I was having a hard time finding **Privilege or Entitlement?** effective Reinforcers and then I realized they received all the Reinforcers they wanted for just showing up. With a transformation of their former entitlements into privileges to be earned, I was able to design a Positive Reinforcement program without having to buy toys or give them unhealthy foods. The Reinforcers were right there in front of me including the TV, computer and video games. I was able to limit how much of this they could consume as they could only earn so much, and they were ever so appreciative and thankful for it when it was earned.

You should be optimistic about Positive Reinforcement. If you made it this far you know more about it than the vast majority of parents, and even some professionals. It's amazing how you will see "professionals" talk about Positive Reinforcement incorrectly. What I see even more of is Negative Reinforcement being described incorrectly. You are knowledgeable and can talk to people with training like teachers, counselors and doctors, and understand what they are doing, what they are doing right and even what they are doing wrong. You are armed with what you need to use Positive Reinforcement with your child and understand how to implement it, track it, measure it, tweak it, and eventually stop doing it and still have your child performing the desired Behavior.

If you still have your doubts, then ask yourself who recommends it and who is against it? You can search the internet for pediatricians who recommend it, and you will find thousands. Ask your own pediatrician what they think of it. You can search psychologist and psychiatrists sites and you will find almost universal support of Positive Reinforcement, and good luck finding a professional who is against it.

Go to this link to see that the American Academy of Pediatrics says about Positive Reinforcement: http://www.healthychildren.org/English/family-life/family-dynamics/Pages/Positive-Reinforcement-Through-Rewards.aspx

I know some people think their kids are too old to use Positive Reinforcement with them. Those same people probably don't know much about Positive Reinforcement and think of it as only sticker charts and don't realize that Positive Reinforcement works on any age person and is routinely used on  adults. Odd are they have a credit card in which they earn points or something in return for performing the Behavior of using that card to pay for a purchase. They probably have some "miles" saved up from their airline or seven out of the ten squares stamped toward a free sub sandwich down at their local eatery. Positive Reinforcement is all around us, and it is in wide use because it is effective.

You should feel good as a Caregiver to have made it this far. You are now prepared to start implementing what you have learned to start replacing undesired Behaviors with desired Behaviors that will improve the life of your child, and you relationship with them. You can feel confident that you have the knowledge and skills to make a positive difference in their life and the life of your family while creating an even deeper bond. As with many things, books are a fantastic learning tool, but can only teach you so much and then you just have to go out and do it. You will make mistakes, but you will know how to fix them, you will get better at doing this and ultimately you will be a better Caregiver for having done it.

Congratulations, you have done a wonderful thing becoming

a better Caregiver and a better person.

Your Children may not thank you right away, or even ever, but you will be rewarded with having raised better, more successful child.

Now go get started today!

GLOSSARY

Activity Reinforcers: Stimuli in the form of activities the child finds to be pleasant that are added with the intent of strengthening a target Behavior.

Alternative schedules: "A type of Compound Schedule where two or more simple schedules are in effect and whichever schedule is completed first results in reinforcement."(*Wikipedia 2011*)

Appetitive stimulus: "Appetitive stimulus = a pleasant outcome" (*Wikipedia 2011*)

Asperger Syndrome: "is an Autism Spectrum Disorder that is characterized by significant difficulties in social interaction, along with restricted and repetitive patterns of behavior and interests. It differs from other Autism Spectrum Disorders by its relative preservation of linguistic and cognitive development. Although not required for diagnosis, physical clumsiness and atypical use of language are frequently reported."(*Wikipedia 2011*)

Aspie: "People identifying with Asperger Syndrome may refer to themselves in casual conversation as aspies, coined by

Liane Holliday Willey in 1999."(*Wikipedia 2011*)

Attention Deficit Hyperactivity Disorder (ADHD): "A developmental disorder in which a person has a persistent pattern of impulsiveness and inattention, with or without a component of hyperactivity." (*Wikipedia 2011*)

Autism (See Autism Spectrum): "is a disorder of neural development characterized by impaired social interaction and communication, and by restricted and repetitive behavior. These signs all begin before a child is three years old.[2] Autism affects information processing in the brain by altering how nerve cells and their synapses connect and organize; how this occurs is not well understood.[3] It is one of three recognized disorders in the autism spectrum (ASDs), the other two being Asperger Syndrome, which lacks delays in cognitive development and language, and Pervasive Developmental Disorder-Not Otherwise Specified (commonly abbreviated as PDD-NOS), which is diagnosed when the full set of criteria for autism or Asperger Syndrome are not met." (*Wikipedia 2011*)

Autism Spectrum (See Autism): "The autism spectrum, also called Autism Spectrum Disorders (ASD) or autism spectrum conditions (ASC), with the adjective autistic sometimes replacing the noun autism, is a spectrum of psychological conditions characterized by widespread abnormalities of social interactions and communication as well as restricted interests and repetitive behaviour."(*Wikipedia 2011*)

Aversive stimulus: "Aversive stimulus = an unpleasant outcome" (*Wikipedia 2011*)

Backwards Chaining: "Chaining involves linking discrete behaviors together in a series, such that each result of each behavior is both the reinforcement (or consequence) for the previous behavior, and the stimuli (or antecedent) for the next behavior. There are many ways to teach Chaining, such as forward Chaining (starting from the first behavior in the chain), backwards Chaining (starting from the last behavior)"(*Wikipedia 2011*)

Behavior: "or behaviour (see American and British spelling differences) refers to the actions of a system or organism, usually in relation to its environment, which includes the other systems or organisms around as well as the physical environment. It is the response of the system or organism to various stimuli or inputs, whether internal or external, conscious or subconscious, overt or covert, and voluntary or involuntary."(*Wikipedia 2011*)

Behaviorism: "(or behaviourism), also called the learning perspective (where any physical action is a behavior), is a philosophy of psychology based on the proposition that all things that organisms do—including acting, thinking and feeling—can and should be regarded as behaviors, and that psychological disorders are best treated by altering behavior patterns.[1][2] The behaviorist school of thought maintains that behaviors as such can be described scientifically without recourse either to internal physiological events or to hypothetical constructs such as the mind.[3] Behaviorism comprises the position that all theories should have observational correlates but that there are no philosophical differences between publicly observable processes (such as actions) and privately observable processes (such as thinking and feeling)."(*Wikipedia 2011*)

Caregivers: For this book the term "Caregivers" as opposed to just Parents, or Parents and Caregivers, or any combination of titles and terms used to cover people who watch or contribute to the raising of children. While not all Caregivers are Parents, all Parents who are involved with their children are Caregivers so that is the term I will go with. If I mean to specify, I will say Parent or Coach or Babysitter or what have you as the situation dictates.

Chaining: "Chaining involves linking discrete behaviors together in a series, such that each result of each behavior is both the reinforcement (or consequence) for the previous behavior, and the stimuli (or antecedent) for the next behavior. There are many ways to teach Chaining, such as forward Chaining (starting from the first behavior in the chain), backwards Chaining (starting from the last behavior)"(*Wikipedia 2011*)

Classical Conditioning: "is a form of Conditioning that was first demonstrated by Ivan Pavlov (1927). The typical procedure for inducing classical Conditioning involves presentations of a neutral stimulus along with a stimulus of some significance, the "Unconditional Stimulus." The neutral stimulus could be any event that does not result in an overt behavioral response from the organism under investigation. Conversely, presentation of the significant stimulus necessarily evokes an innate, often reflexive, response"(*Wikipedia 2011*)

Compound schedules: "combine two or more different simple schedules in some way using the same Reinforcer for the same behavior."(*Wikipedia 2011*)

Conditioned stimulus: In classical Conditioning this is the stimulus that receives a new association by the subject. The conditioned Stimulus is a formerly neutral stimulus that is presented with the Unconditioned Stimulus until the subject associates the two with the same response. In the classic Pavlovian example, the food was shown to a dog who salivated. Next he rang a bell at the same time the food was presented so that the subject (dog) associated the the conditioned stimuli (bell) to the unconditioned stimuli (food) so that both or either created the Unconditioned Response (salivation).

Conditioning: "The process of modifying a person's behaviour."(*Wikipedia 2011*)

Conjunctive schedules: "A complex schedule of reinforcement where two or more simple schedules are in effect independently of each other, and requirements on all of the simple schedules must be met for reinforcement." (*Wikipedia 2011*)

Contiguous stimuli: "are stimuli closely associated by time and space with specific behaviors. They reduce the amount of time needed to learn a behavior while increasing its resistance to extinction. Giving a dog a piece of food immediately after sitting is more contiguous with (and therefore more likely to reinforce) the behavior than a several minute delay in food delivery following the behavior."(*Wikipedia 2011*)

Continuous reinforcement: "a schedule of reinforcement in which every occurrence of the instrumental response produces the Reinforcer" (*Wikipedia 2011*)

Disorder: "A physical or psychical malfunction"(*Wikionary 2011*)

Extinction: "is the Conditioning phenomenon in which a previously learned response to a cue is reduced when the cue is presented in the absence of the previously paired aversive or Appetitive Stimulus." (*Wikipedia 2011*)

Extinction Burst (See Extinction-induced resurgence): "While extinction, when implemented consistently over time, results in the eventual decrease of the undesired behavior, in the short-term the subject might exhibit what is called an

Extinction Burst. An Extinction Burst will often occur when the extinction procedure has just begun. This consists of a sudden and temporary increase in the response's frequency, followed by the eventual decline and extinction of the behavior targeted for elimination." (*Wikipedia 2011*)

Extinction-induced resurgence (See Extinction Burst): "While extinction, when implemented consistently over time, results in the eventual decrease of the undesired behavior, in the short-term the subject might exhibit what is called an Extinction Burst. An Extinction Burst will often occur when the extinction procedure has just begun. This consists of a sudden and temporary increase in the response's frequency, followed by the eventual decline and extinction of the behavior targeted for elimination." (*Wikipedia 2011*)

Extrinsic motivation: "While extinction, when implemented consistently over time, results in the eventual decrease of the undesired behavior, in the short-term the subject might exhibit what is called an Extinction Burst. An Extinction Burst will often occur when the extinction procedure has just begun. This consists of a sudden and temporary increase in the response's frequency, followed by the eventual decline and extinction of the behavior targeted for elimination." (*Wikipedia 2011*)

Fixed interval schedule: "reinforced after every nth amount of time" (*Wikipedia 2011*)

Fixed-ratio schedules: "schedules deliver reinforcement after every nth response" (*Wikipedia 2011*)

Forward Chaining: "Chaining involves linking discrete behaviors together in a series, such that each result of each behavior is both the reinforcement (or consequence) for the previous behavior, and the stimuli (or antecedent) for the next behavior. There are many ways to teach Chaining, such as forward Chaining (starting from the first behavior in the chain), backwards Chaining (starting from the last behavior)" (*Wikipedia 2011*)

Generalized Reinforcers: "is a conditioned Reinforcer that has obtained the Reinforcing function by pairing with many other Reinforcers (such as money, a secondary generalized Reinforcer)." (*Wikipedia 2011*)

Group behavior dependent group reinforcement: Group reinforcement where the program rules and desired behaviors are the same for the whole group and the entire group earns Reinforcers based on the combined behavior of the whole group. Individual performance is lumped together and tracked collectively and that combined metric is used to determine if the group has earned a Reinforcer.

Individual behavior dependent group reinforcement: Group reinforcement where the program rules and desired behaviors are the same for the whole group and the entire group earns Reinforcers based on the collective sum behavior of the individuals in the group. Individual performance is tracked and then used to determine if the group has earned a Reinforcer.

Individual behavior independent group reinforcement: Group reinforcement where the program rules and desired behaviors are the same for the whole group but each child earns their own Reinforcers based solely on their own behavior.

Intermittent reinforcement: "intermittent or partial reinforcement where only some responses are reinforced." (*Wikipedia 2011*)

Intermittent schedules: Reinforcement schedules in which Reinforcers are not given every time a desired behavior is exhibited. Some examples of intermittent schedules include Fixed Ratio, fixed-Interval, variable-interval and variable-ratio.

Interval schedules: Reinforcement schedules in which Reinforcers are given based on an elapsed period of time going by. Both fixed-Interval and variable-interval reinforcement schedules are interval schedules

Intrinsic reinforcement: Reinforcement that the child receives naturally or internally for behaviors. Intrinsic reinforcement can be a result of a child's natural disposition or because of values and beliefs instilled in them.

Law of Effect: "The law of effect basically states that "responses that produce a satisfying effect in a particular situation become more likely to occur again in that situation, and responses that produce a discomforting effect become less likely to occur again in that situation." (*Wikipedia 2011*)

Leader: "One having authority to direct." (*Wikionary 2011*)

Learning Theory: "A Learning Theory is an attempt to describe how people and animals learn, thereby helping us understand the inherently complex process of learning." (*Wikipedia 2011*)

Mixed schedules: "Either of two, or more, schedules may occur with no stimulus indicating which is in force. Reinforcement is delivered if the response requirement is met while a schedule is in effect." (*Wikipedia 2011*)

Multiple schedules: "Two or more schedules alternate over time, with a stimulus indicating which is in force. Reinforcement is delivered if the response requirement is met while a schedule is in effect." (*Wikipedia 2011*)

Natural reinforcement: A form of Intrinsic reinforcement in which the Reinforcer occurs for given behaviors without the need of actions, training or other involvement from forces or people outside the child.

Negative Punishment: "the taking away of an Appetitive Stimulus to decrease a certain behavior. Example: A teenager comes home an hour after curfew and the parents take away the teen's cell phone for two days. If the frequency of coming home after curfew decreases, the removal of the phone is negative punishment." (*Wikipedia 2011*)

Negative Punishment for Children: The removal of a result or consequence that the child finds pleasant, dependent on the occurrence of a certain behavior or response by the child, which results in a decrease in the likelihood of that behavior or response in the child, because of the removed result or consequence.

Negative reinforcement: "the taking away of an Aversive Stimulus to increase certain behavior or response. Example: Turning off distracting music when trying to work. If the work increases when the music is turned off, turning off the music is a negative Reinforcer." (*Wikipedia 2011*)

Negative Reinforcement for Kids: The removal of a result or consequence that the child finds unpleasant, dependent on the occurrence of a certain behavior or response by the child, which results in an increase in the likelihood of that behavior or response in the child, because of the removed result or consequence.

Operant Chamber (See Skinner Box): "An Operant Conditioning chamber (also known as the Skinner Box) is a laboratory apparatus used in the experimental analysis of behavior to study animal behavior." (*Wikipedia 2011*)

Operant Conditioning: "is a form of psychological learning where an individual modifies the occurrence and form of its own behavior due to the association of the behavior with a stimulus. Operant Conditioning is distinguished from classical Conditioning (also called respondent Conditioning) in that Operant Conditioning deals with the modification of "voluntary behavior" or Operant behavior" (*Wikipedia 2011*)

Persistence (See Resistance to extinction): The characteristic of reinforcement in which the subject will continue to exhibit the desired behavior even in the occasional absence of a Reinforcer. The more the subject will exhibit the desired behavior without being reinforced the more resistant the reinforcement is said to be. Extinction being the reduction in the exhibition of the behavior in the absence of a Reinforcer.

Positive Punishment: "the adding of an Aversive Stimulus to decrease a certain behavior or response. Example: Mother yells at a child when running into the street. If the child stops running into the street the yelling is punishment." (*Wikipedia 2011*)

Positive Punishment for Children: The adding of a result or consequence that the child finds unpleasant, dependent on the occurrence of a certain behavior or response by the child, which results in a decrease in the likelihood of that behavior or response in the child, because of the added result or consequence.

Positive reinforcement: "the adding of an Appetitive Stimulus to increase a certain behavior or response. Example: Father gives candy to his daughter when she picks up her toys. If the frequency of picking up the toys increases or stays the same, the candy is a positive Reinforcer." (*Wikipedia 2011*)

Positive Reinforcement for Kids: The adding of a result or consequence that the child finds pleasant, dependent on the occurrence of a certain behavior or response by the child, which results in an increase in the likelihood of that behavior or response in the child, because of the added result or consequence.

Premack principle: "(Premack, 1959, 1963) states that more probable behaviors will reinforce less probable behaviors." (*Wikipedia 2011*)

Primary Reinforcer: "A primary Reinforcer, sometimes called an unconditioned Reinforcer, is a stimulus that does not require pairing to function as a Reinforcer and most likely has obtained this function through the evolution and its role in species' survival" (*Wikipedia 2011*)

Punisher: A Reinforcer presented after a specific behavior that decreases the frequency of the behavior actually.

Punishment: "is any change in a human or animal's surroundings that occurs after a given behavior or response which reduces the likelihood of that behavior occurring again in the future." (*Wikipedia 2011*)

Puzzle box: Used by Edward L. Thondike. "The puzzle box consisted of a lever or a loop that could open the door, thereby releasing the hungry cat to freedom and to the food placed just outside the box." (*Wikipedia 2011*)

Radical Behaviorism: "is a philosophy developed by B.F. Skinner that underlies the experimental analysis of behavior approach to psychology." (*Wikipedia 2011*)

Ratio schedules: "the reinforcement depends only on the number of responses the organism has performed" (*Wikipedia 2011*)

Reinforcement: "is a term in Operant Conditioning and behavior analysis for the process of increasing the rate or probability of a behavior (e.g., pulling a lever more frequently) in the form of a "response" by the delivery or emergence of a stimulus (e.g. a candy) immediately or shortly after performing the behavior." (*Wikipedia 2011*)

Reinforcement schedules: "A schedule of reinforcement is a rule or program that determines how and when the occurrence of a response will be followed by the delivery of the Reinforcer, and extinction, in which no response is reinforced." (*Wikipedia 2011*)

Reinforcer: The stimuli that are added with the intent of strengthening a target Behavior.

Resistance to extinction (See Persistence) : The characteristic of reinforcement in which the subject will continue to exhibit the desired behavior even in the occasional absence of a Reinforcer. The more the subject will exhibit the desired behavior without being reinforced the more resistant the reinforcement is said to be. Extinction being the reduction in the exhibition of the behavior in the absence of a Reinforcer.

Response: Any behavior in reaction to a stimuli.

Satiation: is what we call it when a Reinforcer starts to loose its effectiveness, which may cause extinction to begin.

Schedule: "A timetable, or other time-based plan of events; a plan of what is to occur, and at what time." (*Wikionary 2011*)

Schedules of Reinforcement: "A schedule of reinforcement is a rule or program that determines how and when the occurrence of a response will be followed by the delivery of the Reinforcer, and extinction, in which no response is reinforced" (*Wikipedia 2011*)

Secondary Reinforcers: "A secondary Reinforcer, sometimes called a conditioned Reinforcer, is a stimulus or situation that has acquired its function as a Reinforcer after pairing with a stimulus that functions as a Reinforcer." (*Wikipedia 2011*)

Sensory Reinforcers: Stimuli the child finds to be pleasant to the senses such as smell, taste, sound, feel or look, that are added with the intent of strengthening a target Behavior.

Shaping: "The differential reinforcement of successive approximations, or more commonly, Shaping is a Conditioning procedure used primarily in the experimental analysis of behavior." (*Wikipedia 2011*)

Skinner Box (See Operant Chamber) : "An Operant Conditioning chamber (also known as the Skinner Box) is a laboratory apparatus used in the experimental analysis of behavior to study animal behavior." (*Wikipedia 2011*)

Social Reinforcers: Stimuli in the form of interactions with, or recognition from, other people that the child finds to be pleasant that are added with the intent of strengthening a target Behavior.

Spontaneous Recovery: "is a phenomenon first seen in Pavlovian Conditioning and then later discovered in memory functioning. The general pattern of Spontaneous Recovery found in Pavlovian Conditioning in animals essentially encompasses two varying habits learned by the animal where there is an initial overpowering presence of habit 2 over habit 1 and then over time, habit 1 regains empowerment over habit 2. This is parallel to learning in human memory." (*Wikipedia 2011*)

Stimulus: "In Behaviorism and related stimulus–response theories, stimuli constitute the basis for behavior" (*Wikipedia 2011*)

Subgroup Behavior Dependent Group Reinforcement: Group reinforcement where the program rules and desired behaviors apply only to the subgroup (or individual) but the entire group earns Reinforcers based on the behavior of the subgroup (or individual).

Tangible Reinforcers: Stimuli in the form of physical items that the child finds to be pleasant that are added with the intent of strengthening a target Behavior.

Token Economy: "A Token Economy is a system of behavior modification based on the systematic positive reinforcement of target behavior." (*Wikipedia 2011*)

Tokens: "A Token is an object or symbol that can be exchanged for material Reinforcers, services or privileges (back-up Reinforcers)." (*Wikipedia 2011*)

Unconditional Stimulus: "The neutral stimulus could be any event that does not result in an overt behavioral response from the organism under investigation." (*Wikipedia 2011*)

Variable Interval Schedule: "reinforced on an average every nth amount of time. the 'n' is an average." (*Wikipedia 2011*)

Variable ratio schedules: "a reinforcement schedule in which the number of responses necessary to produce reinforcement varies from trial to trial." (*Wikipedia 2011*)

Variable Schedules: Reinforcement schedule that varies based on number of time the behavior is exhibited or by the passage of time to a degree that it may appear random to the subject of the reinforcement.

WORKS CITED

"Asperger Syndrome - Wikipedia, the free encyclopedia." *Wikipedia, the free encyclopedia.* N.p., n.d. Web. 22 Aug. 2011. <http://en.wikipedia.org/wiki/Asperger_Syndrome>.

"Attention deficit hyperactivity disorder - Wikipedia, the free encyclopedia." *Wikipedia, the free encyclopedia.* N.p., n.d. Web. 22 Aug. 2011. <http://en.wikipedia.org/wiki/Attention_Deficit_Hyperactivity_Disorder>.

"attention deficit hyperactivity disorder - Wiktionary.." *Wiktionary, the free dictionary.* N.p., n.d. Web. 12 Aug. 2011. <en.wiktionary.org/wiki/attention_deficit_hyperactivity_disorder>.

"Autism - Wikipedia, the free encyclopedia." *Wikipedia, the free encyclopedia.* N.p., n.d. Web. 22 Aug. 2011. <http://en.wikipedia.org/wiki/Autism>.

"Autism spectrum - Wikipedia, the free encyclopedia." *Wikipedia, the free encyclopedia.* N.p., n.d. Web. 22 Aug. 2011. <http://en.wikipedia.org/wiki/Autism_spectrum>.

"B. F. Skinner - Wikipedia, the free encyclopedia." *Wikipedia, the free encyclopedia.* N.p., n.d. Web. 18 Sept. 2011. <http://en.wikipedia.org/wiki/BF_Skinner>.

"Backward Chaining | in Chapter 05: Conditioning | from Psychology: An Introduction by Russ Dewey." *Psych Web by Russ Dewey.* N.p., n.d. Web. 18 Apr. 2011. <http://www.psywww.com/intropsych/ch05_Conditi oning/backward_Chaining.html>.

"Behavior - Wikipedia, the free encyclopedia." *Wikipedia, the free encyclopedia.* N.p., n.d. Web. 22 Aug. 2011. <http://en.wikipedia.org/wiki/Behavior>.

"Behaviorism - Wikipedia, the free encyclopedia." *Wikipedia, the free encyclopedia.* N.p., n.d. Web. 22 Aug. 2011. <http://en.wikipedia.org/wiki/Behaviorism>.

"Changing Behavior Through Reinforcement and Punishment: Operant Conditioning | Flat World Knowledge." *Welcome | Flat World Knowledge.* N.p., n.d. Web. 18 Sept. 2011. <http://www.flatworldknowledge.com/pub/introduction-psychology/67091#web-67091>.

"Child Positive Reinforcement " 3 Studies That Say It™s BAD! | Parenting Tips For Raising Successful Kids | BetterParenting.com." *Parenting Tips For Raising Successful Kids | BetterParenting.com | Find A Plethora of Parenting Tips & Tricks To Help Your Children Succeed and Make Your Life Easier..* N.p., n.d. Web. 18 Sept. 2011. <http://www.betterparenting.com/child-positive-reinforcement/>.

"Classical Conditioning - Wikipedia, the free encyclopedia." *Wikipedia, the free encyclopedia.* N.p., n.d. Web. 31 Aug. 2011.

<http://en.wikipedia.org/wiki/Classical_Conditioning

>.

"Conditioning - Wiktionary." *Wiktionary, the free dictionary.* N.p., n.d. Web. 25 Aug. 2011. <http://en.wiktionary.org/wiki/Conditioning>.

"Discriminative Stimuli | in Chapter 05: Conditioning | from Psychology: An Introduction by Russ Dewey." *Psych Web by Russ Dewey.* N.p., n.d. Web. 18 Sept. 2011. <http://www.psywww.com/intropsych/ch05_Conditi oning/discriminative_stimuli.html>.

"disorder - Wiktionary." *Wiktionary, the free dictionary.* N.p., n.d. Web. 25 Aug. 2011. <http://en.wiktionary.org/wiki/disorder>.

"Educational Psychology Interactive: Operant Conditioning." *Educational Psychology Interactive.* N.p., n.d. Web. 18 Sept. 2011. <http://www.edpsycinteractive.org/topics/behavior/ Operant.html>.

"Edward Thorndike - Wikipedia, the free encyclopedia." *Wikipedia, the free encyclopedia.* N.p., n.d. Web. 18 Sept. 2011.

<http://en.wikipedia.org/wiki/Edward_Thorndike>.

"Extinction (psychology) - Wikipedia, the free encyclopedia." *Wikipedia, the free encyclopedia.* N.p., n.d. Web. 25 Aug. 2011.

<http://en.wikipedia.org/wiki/Extinction_(psycholog y)#Extinction_burst>.

"Extinction of an Operant Response | in Chapter 05: Conditioning | from Psychology: An Introduction by Russ Dewey." *Psych Web by Russ Dewey.* N.p., n.d. Web. 18 Sept. 2011. <http://www.psywww.com/intropsych/ch05_Conditi oning/extinction_of_an_Operant_response.html>.

"Extinction-Induced Resurgence (the "Extinction Burst") | in Chapter 05: Conditioning | from Psychology: An Introduction by Russ Dewey." *Psych Web by Russ*

Dewey. N.p., n.d. Web. 18 Sept. 2011. <http://www.psywww.com/intropsych/ch05_Conditi oning/extinction_burst.html>.

Ferster, C. B., and B. F. Skinner. *Schedules of Reinforcement, by C. B. Ferster and B. F. Skinner.*. New York: Appleton-Century-Crofts, 1957. Print.

"Harvard Education Letter." *Harvard Education Publishing Group.* N.p., n.d. Web. 18 Sept. 2011. <http://hepg.org/hel/article/463>.

"Intermittent Reinforcement and Resistance to Extinction | in Chapter 05: Conditioning | from Psychology: An Introduction by Russ Dewey." *Psych Web by Russ Dewey.* N.p., n.d. Web. 18 Sept. 2011. <http://www.psywww.com/intropsych/ch05_Conditi oning/intermittent_reinforcement.html>.

"John B. Watson - Wikipedia, the free encyclopedia." *Wikipedia, the free encyclopedia.* N.p., n.d. Web. 18 Sept. 2011.

<http://en.wikipedia.org/wiki/John_B._Watson>.

Kohn, Alfie. "Five Reasons to Stop Saying "Good Job!"." *Alfie Kohn author teacher lecturer www.alfiekohn.org*. N.p., n.d. Web. 18 Sept. 2011. <http://www.alfiekohn.org/parenting/gj.htm>.

Kohn, Alfie. "The Risks of Rewards." *Alfie Kohn author teacher lecturer www.alfiekohn.org*. N.p., n.d. Web. 18 Sept. 2011. <http://www.alfiekohn.org/teaching/ror.htm>.

Kohn, Alfie. *Punished by rewards: the trouble with gold stars, incentive plans, A's, praise, and other bribes*. Boston: Houghton Mifflin Co., 1993. Print.

"Law of effect - Wikipedia, the free encyclopedia." *Wikipedia, the free encyclopedia*. N.p., n.d. Web. 28 Aug. 2011. <en.wikipedia.org/wiki/Law_of_Effect>.

"leader - Wiktionary." *Wiktionary, the free dictionary*. . N.p., n.d. Web. 28 Aug. 2011. <en.wiktionary.org/wiki/leader>.

"Learning Theory (education) - Wikipedia, the free

encyclopedia." *Wikipedia, the free encyclopedia.* N.p., n.d. Web. 28 Aug. 2011. <http://en.wikipedia.org/wiki/Learning_theory_(edu cation)>.

Logsdon, Â Ann. "Positive Reinforcers - Easy Ways to Reinforce Positive Behavior in Children." *Learning Disability - What is a Learning Disability?*. N.p., n.d. Web. 18 Sept. 2011. <http://learningdisabilities.about.com/od/behaviorpr oblems/p/Reinforcers.htm>.

"Negative Reinforcement | in Chapter 05: Conditioning | from Psychology: An Introduction by Russ Dewey." *Psych Web by Russ Dewey.* N.p., n.d. Web. 18 Sept. 2011. <http://www.psywww.com/intropsych/ch05_Conditi oning/negative_reinforcement.html>.

"News For Parents.org - Positive Reinforcement and Autism." *News For Parents .org - Parenting News and Information.* N.p., n.d. Web. 18 Sept. 2011.

<http://www.newsforparents.org/expert_autism_rein forcement.html>.

"Operant Conditioning - Wikipedia, the free encyclopedia." *Wikipedia, the free encyclopedia.* N.p., n.d. Web. 29 Aug. 2011.

<http://en.wikipedia.org/wiki/Operant_Conditioning >.

"Operant Conditioning chamber - Wikipedia, the free encyclopedia." *Wikipedia, the free encyclopedia.* N.p., n.d. Web. 29 Aug. 2011. <http://en.wikipedia.org/wiki/Skinner_box>.

Ormrod, Jeanne Ellis. *Educational psychology: developing learners.* 4th ed., Multimedia ed. Upper Saddle River, NJ: Merrill/Prentice Hall, 2003. Print.

"outcome - Wiktionary." *Wiktionary, the free dictionary.* N.p., n.d. Web. 28 Aug. 2011. <http://en.wiktionary.org/wiki/outcome>.

"Premack's principle - Wikipedia, the free encyclopedia." *Wikipedia, the free encyclopedia.* N.p., n.d. Web. 29 Aug. 2011.
<http://en.wikipedia.org/wiki/Premack_principle>.

" Positive Reinforcement and Negative - Classical And Operant Conditioning - Response, Stimulus, Thorndike, Conditioned, Food, and Powder." *Science Encyclopedia.* N.p., n.d. Web. 18 Sept. 2011. <http://science.jrank.org/pages/5781/Reinforcement-Positive-Negative-Classical-Operant-Conditioning.html>.

"Positive Reinforcement and Negative - Reinforcement Schedules - Interval, Ratio, Responses, Response, Reinforced, and Behaviors." *Science Encyclopedia.* N.p., n.d. Web. 18 Sept. 2011. <http://science.jrank.org/pages/5782/Reinforcement-Positive-Negative-Reinforcement-schedules.html>.

"Positive Reinforcement - WikEd." *Main Page - WikEd.* N.p., n.d. Web. 18 Sept. 2011. <http://wik.ed.uiuc.edu/index.php/Positive_Reinforc ement>.

"Positive Reinforcement Tutorial : Centre for Psychology : Athabasca University." *Centre for Psychology : Faculty of Humanities and Social Sciences : Athabasca University.* N.p., n.d. Web. 18 Sept. 2011. <http://psych.athabascau.ca/html/prtut/>.

"Punishment (psychology) - Wikipedia, the free encyclopedia." *Wikipedia, the free encyclopedia.* N.p., n.d. Web. 29 Aug. 2011. <http://en.wikipedia.org/wiki/Punishment_(psycholo gy)>.

"Radical Behaviorism - Wikipedia, the free encyclopedia." *Wikipedia, the free encyclopedia.* N.p., n.d. Web. 29 Aug. 2011. <http://en.wikipedia.org/wiki/Radical_Behaviorism>.

"Reinforcement - Wikipedia, the free encyclopedia." *Wikipedia, the free encyclopedia*. N.p., n.d. Web. 18 Sept. 2011. <http://en.wikipedia.org/wiki/Reinforcement>.

"Reinforcement and Punishment." *Department of Psychology - The University of Iowa*. N.p., n.d. Web. 18 Sept. 2011. <http://www.psychology.uiowa.edu/faculty/wasserm an/glossary/reinforcement.html>.

"Reinforcement and Punishment in Psychology 101 at AllPsych Online." *Psychology Classroom at AllPsych Online*. N.p., n.d. Web. 18 Sept. 2011. <http://allpsych.com/psychology101/reinforcement.ht ml>.

"Reinforcement and Punishment in Psychology 101 at AllPsych Online." *Psychology Classroom at AllPsych Online*. N.p., n.d. Web. 18 Sept. 2011. <http://allpsych.com/psychology101/reinforcement.ht ml>.

"Response Cost ("Negative Punishment") | in Chapter 05: Conditioning | from Psychology: An Introduction by

Russ Dewey." *Psych Web by Russ Dewey.* N.p., n.d. Web. 18 Sept. 2011. <http://www.psywww.com/intropsych/ch05_Conditioning/response_cost.html>.

Sanders, April. "How to Use Positive Reinforcement in the Classroom | eHow.com." *eHow | How to Videos, Articles & More - Trusted Advice for the Curious Life | eHow.com.* N.p., n.d. Web. 18 Sept. 2011. <http://www.ehow.com/how_4556420_use-positive-reinforcement-classroom.html>.

"Scenarios for Using Behaviorism - Emerging Perspectives on Learning, Teaching and Technology." *Projects Server Introduction.* N.p., n.d. Web. 18 Sept. 2011. <http://projects.coe.uga.edu/epltt/index.php?title=Scenarios_for_Using_Behaviorism>.

"schedule - Wiktionary." *Wiktionary, the free dictionary.* N.p., n.d. Web. 29 Aug. 2011. <http://en.wiktionary.org/wiki/schedule>.

"Shaping (psychology) - Wikipedia, the free encyclopedia." *Wikipedia, the free encyclopedia.* N.p., n.d. Web. 29 Aug. 2011. <http://en.wikipedia.org/wiki/Shaping_(psychology)>.

"Skinner - Operant Conditioning." *Psychology Articles for A-level and Degree Study.* N.p., n.d. Web. 18 Sept. 2011. <http://www.simplypsychology.org/Operant-Conditioning.html>.

Skinner, B. F.. *The behavior of organisms; an experimental analysis,.* New York, London: D. Appleton-Century Company, Incorporated, 1938. Print.

Skinner, B. F.. *About Behaviorism.* [1st ed. New York: Knopf; [Distributed By Random House], 1974. Print.

Skinner, B. F.. *Walden Two.* New York: Macmillan, 1976. Print.

Skinner, B. F., and Robert Epstein. *Skinner for the classroom: selected papers.* Champaign: Research Press, 1982.

Print.

"Special Connections." *Special Connections - Home*. N.p., n.d. Web. 18 Sept. 2011. <http://www.specialconnections.ku.edu/cgi-bin/cgiwrap/specconn/main.php?cat=behavior&section=main&subsection=classroom/positive>.

"Spontaneous Recovery - Wikipedia, the free encyclopedia." *Wikipedia, the free encyclopedia*. N.p., n.d. Web. 31 Aug. 2011. <http://en.wikipedia.org/wiki/Spontaneous_recovery>.

"Stimulus - Wikipedia, the free encyclopedia." *Wikipedia, the free encyclopedia*. N.p., n.d. Web. 31 Aug. 2011. <http://en.wikipedia.org/wiki/Stimulus>.

"Teaching Positive Reinforcement." *What To Expect When You're Expecting, Pregnancy, Baby, Babies, Toddler, Parenting -- WhatToExpect.com*. N.p., n.d. Web. 18 Sept. 2011. <http://www.whattoexpect.com/toddler-

behavior/teaching-positive-reinforcement.aspx>.

"The Premack Principle I in Chapter 05: Conditioning I from Psychology: An Introduction by Russ Dewey." *Psych Web by Russ Dewey*. N.p., n.d. Web. 18 Sept. 2011. <http://www.psywww.com/intropsych/ch05_Conditi oning/premack_principle.html>.

"Token Economy - Wikipedia, the free encyclopedia." *Wikipedia, the free encyclopedia*. N.p., n.d. Web. 31 Aug. 2011.

<http://en.wikipedia.org/wiki/Token_economy>.

Vize, Â Anne. "Positive Reinforcement as a Special Education Teaching Strategy." *Find Science & Technology Articles, Education Lesson Plans, Tech Tips, Computer Hardware & Software Reviews, News and More at Bright Hub*. N.p., n.d. Web. 18 Sept. 2011. <http://www.brighthub.com/education/special/article s/41325.aspx>.

"What is Negative Reinforcement?." *Maricopa Center for*

Learning and Instruction | *Maricopa Center for Learning and Instruction*. N.p., n.d. Web. 18 Sept. 2011. <http://www.mcli.dist.maricopa.edu/proj/nru/nr.html >.

"Why Positive Reinforcement doesn't seem to work. (article)." *Articles on how to feel good more often and get more done.* . N.p., n.d. Web. 18 Sept. 2011. <http://www.youmeworks.com/wprdstw.html>.

MLA formatting by BibMe.org.

PICTURE BIBLIOGRAPHY

Alexander , Billy. Coloring Stuff 3 . N.d. Photograph, Freephotos. Web. 23 Mar. 2011.

BOULANGER , Martin. interview. N.d. Photograph, Freephotos. Web. 26 Mar. 2011.

Balch , Charlie. Feed the children 4. N.d. Photograph, Freephotos. Web. 4 Mar. 2011.

Braswell , S. The boys. N.d. Photograph, Freephotos. Web. 28 Mar. 2011.

Chernyshevych , Artem. Shiny brain. N.d. Photograph, Freephotos. Web. 8 Apr. 2011.

Cliver, CP. Graphic-Using Shaping to mold-4. N.d. Graphic, Positive Reinforcement For Kids. Web. 26 Mar. 2011.

Cliver, CP. Pros and Cons of Different Reinforcement Schedules. N.d. Graphic, Positive Reinforcement For Kids. Web. 22 Mar. 2011.

Cliver, CP. Positive Reinforcement, should be used . N.d. Graphic, Positive Reinforcement For Kids. Web. 27 Apr. 2011.

Cliver, CP. Positive Reinforcement is sometimes. N.d. Graphic, Positive Reinforcement For Kids. Web. 26 Mar. 2011.

Cliver, CP. Operant Conditioning. N.d. Graphic, Positive Reinforcement For Kids. Web. 16 Mar. 2011.

Cliver, CP. Working Definitions 2. N.d. Graphic, Positive Reinforcement For Kids. Web. 18 Apr. 2011.

Cliver, CP. Just trying is often. N.d. Graphic, Positive Reinforcement For Kids. Web. 10 Apr. 2011.

Cliver, CP. TB-CHAPTER 1 QUIZ ANSWER-5. N.d. Graphic, Positive Reinforcement For Kids. Web. 4 Apr. 2011.

Cliver, CP. TB-CHAPTER 1 QUIZ ANSWER-4. N.d. Graphic, Positive Reinforcement For Kids. Web. 4 Apr. 2011.

Cliver, CP. The consequences of. N.d. Graphic, Positive Reinforcement For Kids. Web. 26 Apr. 2011.

Cliver, CP. TB-CHAPTER 1 QUIZ ANSWER-3 . N.d. Graphic, Positive Reinforcement For Kids. Web. 4 Apr. 2011.

Cliver, CP. TB-CHAPTER 1 QUIZ ANSWER-2. N.d. Graphic, Positive Reinforcement For Kids. Web. 4 Apr. 2011.

Cliver, CP. TB-CHAPTER 1 QUIZ ANSWER-1. N.d. Graphic, Positive Reinforcement For Kids. Web. 4 Apr. 2011.

Cliver, CP. TB-Behavior Goals 2. N.d. Graphic, Positive Reinforcement For Kids. Web. 16 Apr. 2011.

Cliver, CP. TB-Behavior Goals 1. N.d. Graphic, Positive Reinforcement For Kids. Web. 6 Mar. 2011.

Cliver, CP. Basic Steps of a Positive Reinforcement Program. N.d. Graphic, Positive Reinforcement For Kids. Web. 5 Apr. 2011.

Cliver, CP. Asperger Definition. N.d. Graphic, Positive Reinforcement For Kids. Web. 3 Mar. 2011.

Cliver, CP. ADHD Definintion. N.d. Graphic, Positive Reinforcement For Kids. Web. 2 Mar. 2011.

Cliver, CP. Milkshake Joy. N.d. Photograph, Cover Art. Positive Reinforcement For Kids. Web. 6 Nov. 2010.

Cliver, CP. Variable Ratio Schedule. N.d. Graphic, Positive Reinforcement For Kids. Web. 1 Apr. 2011.

Cliver, CP. Variable Interval Schedule. N.d. Graphic, Positive Reinforcement For Kids. Web. 26 Mar. 2011.

Cliver, CP. Extinction. N.d. Graphic, Positive Reinforcement For Kids. Web. 26 Mar. 2011.

Cliver, CP. Questions for Group Positive Reinforcement. N.d. Graphic, Positive Reinforcement For Kids. Web. 9 Apr. 2011.

Cliver, CP. Graphic-Using Shaping to mold-3. N.d. Graphic, Positive Reinforcement For Kids. Web. 26 Mar. 2011.

Cliver, CP. Graphic-Using Shaping to mold-2. N.d. Graphic , Positive Reinforcement For Kids. Web. 26 Mar. 2011.

Cliver, CP. Using Shaping to mold-1. N.d. Graphic, Positive Reinforcement For Kids. Web. 26 Mar. 2011.

Cliver, CP. Tracking chart. N.d. Graphic, Positive Reinforcement For Kids. Web. 11 Mar. 2011.

Cliver, CP. Ticket Chart. N.d. Graphic, Positive Reinforcement For Kids. Web. 3 Apr. 2011.

Cliver, CP. student driver. N.d. Graphic, Positive Reinforcement For Kids. Web. 9 Mar. 2011.

Cliver, CP. Star. N.d. Graphic , Positive Reinforcement For Kids. Web. 16 Apr. 2011.

Cliver, CP. Satiation. N.d. Graphic, Positive Reinforcement For Kids. Web. 17 Apr. 2011.

Cliver, CP. Reinforcement Schedules . N.d. Graphic, Positive Reinforcement For Kids. Web. 30 Mar. 2011.

Cliver, CP. Quote-Positive Reinforcement . N.d. Graphic,

Positive Reinforcement For Kids. Web. 28 Mar. 2011.

Cliver, CP. Privilege or entitlement. N.d. Graphic, Positive Reinforcement For Kids. Web. 25 Apr. 2011.

Cliver, CP. TIP: Hand one. N.d. Graphic, Positive Reinforcement For Kids. Web. 10 Mar. 2011.

Cliver, CP. Working Definitions 1. N.d. Graphic, Positive Reinforcement For Kids. Web. 2 Apr. 2011.

Cliver, CP. Positive Reinforcement is flexible. N.d. Graphic, Positive Reinforcement For Kids. Web. 13 Mar. 2011.

Cliver, CP. No to Good Job. N.d. Graphic, Positive Reinforcement For Kids. Web. 4 Apr. 2011.

Cliver, CP. KISS. N.d. Graphic, Positive Reinforcement For Kids . Web. 23 Apr. 2011.

Cliver, CP. Fixed Ratio Schedule. N.d. Graphic, Positive Reinforcement For Kids. Web. 22 Mar. 2011.

Cliver, CP. Fixed Interval Schedule. N.d. Graphic, Positive Reinforcement For Kids. Web. 21 Apr. 2011.

Cliver, CP. Extinction Burst. N.d. Graphic, Positive Reinforcement For Kids. Web. 15 Mar. 2011.

Cliver, CP. ABCD. N.d. Graphic, Positive Reinforcement For Kids. Web. 22 Mar. 2011.

Cliver, CP. ADHD. N.d. Graphic, Positive Reinforcement For Kids. Web. 22 Apr. 2011.

Cliver, CP. Behavior Opportunity Tracking. N.d. Chart, Positive Reinforcement For Kids. Web. 25 Mar. 2011.

Cliver, CP. Be good for the babysitter. N.d. Graphic , Positive Reinforcement For Kids. Web. 22 Mar. 2011.

Cliver, CP. Behaviorsaurus. N.d. Graphic, Positive Reinforcement For Kids. Web. 6 Apr. 2011.

Cliver, CP. Chaining. N.d. Graphic, Positive Reinforcement For Kids. Web. 17 Apr. 2011.

Cliver, CP. Clean room. N.d. Chart, Positive Reinforcement For Kids. Web. 2 May 2011.

Cliver, CP. Continuous Reinforcement schedule. N.d. Graphic, Positive Reinforcement For Kids. Web. 26 Mar. 2011.

Cliver, CP. Graphic-Using Shaping to mold-5. N.d. Graphic, Positive Reinforcement For Kids. Web. 26 Mar. 2011.

Cliver, CP. Leaning Theory. 2011. Chart, Positive Reinforcement For Kids. Web. 22 Feb. 2011.

DeVries , Sarah. Kiddies Soccer. N.d. Photograph, Freephotos. Web. 2 May 2011.

Diaz Aravena, Rodrigo. Baloo 1 2. N.d. Photograph, Freephotos. Web. 1 Feb. 2011.

Freeman-Woolpert , Julia. Whistle. N.d. Photograph, Freephotos. Web. 16 Mar. 2011.

Gober , Mary. Cap & Diploma. N.d. Photograph, Freephotos. Web. 25 Mar. 2011.

Goodwin , Steven. Dollar sign . N.d. Photograph, Freephotos. Web. 24 Feb. 2011.

Gwarek , Dominik. Feedback form: excellent. N.d. Photograph, Freephotos. Web. 8 Mar. 2011.

Howson , Oli. screwdriver. N.d. Photograph, Freephotos. Web. 6 Mar. 2011.

Mcinnes , Gary. Ticked Checkbox . N.d. Photograph,

Freephotos. Web. .

Medrano , Diego. gummys. N.d. Photograph, Freephotos. Web. 23 Apr. 2011.

Milev , Svilen. Take the buck 1. N.d. Photograph, Freephotos. Web. 16 Mar. 2011.

Milev , Svilen. Winner's podium 2. N.d. Photograph, Freephotos. Web. 23 Feb. 2011.

Prole , Ivan. Puzzle shape. N.d. Photograph, Freephotos. Web. 22 Mar. 2011.

Prole , Ivan. Clock . N.d. Photograph, Freephotos. Web. 21 Mar. 2011.

Pupo Rodrigues , Celso. Quinta da Boa Vista 7. N.d. Photograph, Freephotos. Web. 15 Apr. 2011.

Retreage , Oscar. Mexican-babies. N.d. Photograph, Freephotos.com. Web. 6 Apr. 2011.

Riesen , Guillaume. 20-Sided Dice 2 . N.d. Photograph, Freephotos. Web. .

Rolf , T.. Crybaby . N.d. Photograph, Freephotos. Web. 26 Mar. 2011.

Rollo , Jenny. Waiting and Watching. N.d. Photograph, Freephotos. Web. 14 Mar. 2011.

Romero , Alfonso. THEY FIRST SCHOOL. N.d. Photograph, Freephotos. Web. 6 Apr. 2011.

Stadler , William. Washing hands . N.d. Photograph, Freephotos. Web. 23 Jan. 2011.

Stengel , Jacque. Bus. N.d. Photograph, Freephotos. Web. 15 Feb. 2011.

Sveda , Bina. Teens. N.d. Photograph, Freephotos. Web. 16 Mar. 2011.

Szerpicki , Tiffany. Doodled desks 2 . N.d. Photograph, Freephotos. Web. .

Szkurlatowski , Kriss. Be together 3. N.d. Photograph, Freephotos. Web. 2 May 2011.

Tabata , Jarin. gumball machines. N.d. Photograph, Freephotos. Web. 9 Mar. 2011.

Tainton , Stephen. Jelly Beans 2. N.d. Photograph, Freephotos. Web. 7 Feb. 2011.

Ufniak , Michal. Measuring tape . N.d. Photograph, Freephotos. Web. 16 Feb. 2011.

VillÃ©n , Alberto. Tres_caracoles. N.d. Photograph, Freephotos. Web. 21 Apr. 2011.

Volckaert , Lieven. Scream. N.d. Photograph, Freephotos. Web. 2 Mar. 2011.

unknown , unknown . KD. N.d. Photograph, Freephotos. Web. 16 Mar. 2011.

unknown , unknown . Check list . N.d. Photograph, Freephotos. Web. 14 Mar. 2011.

unknown , unknown . Plato . N.d. Photograph, Freephotos. Web. 2 May 2011.

unknown , unknown . Small young scouts . N.d. Photograph, Freephotos. Web. 8 Mar. 2011.

unknown , unknown . Apple . N.d. Photograph, Freephotos. Web. 20 Apr. 2011.

unknown , unknown . Watson . N.d. Photograph. National

Library of Medicine,

unknown , unknown . Pavlov . N.d. Photograph, Wikipedia . Web. 28 Mar. 2011.

unknown , unknown . Thorndike. N.d. Photograph. Image Courtesy of the National Library of Medicine,

unknown , unknown . But I want it!. N.d. Photograph, Freephotos. Web. 23 Feb. 2011.

unknown , unknown . Skinner. N.d. Photograpgh, Wikipedia. Web. 12 May 2011.

unknown, unknown. Creditcard. N.d. Photograph,. Freephotos. Web. 11 Mar. 2011.

unknown, unknown. plane 1. N.d. Photograph, Freephotos. Web. 20 Mar. 2011.

INDEX

R

S